Co

MW01282028

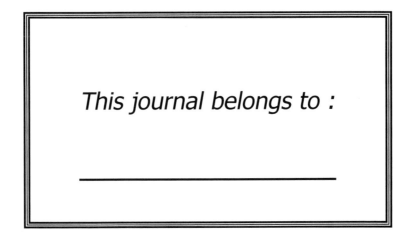

This journal belongs to :

_____

© The Cookbook Publisher 2017

This publication is protected by copyright.

All rights reserved. No part of this publication may be reproduced or transmitted in any form or by any means, electronic or mechanical, including photocopying, recording, or any other information storage and retrieval system without the written permission from the copyright owner.

Disclaimer and Terms of Use

Efforts have been made to ensure that the information in this journal is accurate and complete. However, the author and the publisher do not warrant the accuracy of the information, text, and graphics contained within the journal due to the rapidly changing nature of science, research, known and unknown facts, and the internet. The author and the publisher do not hold any responsibility for errors, omissions, or contrary interpretation of the subject matter herein. This journal is presented solely for motivational and informational purposes only. The author and publisher do not take any responsibility for any consequences that may result due to following the instructions provided in this journal.

Please consult your physician before making any changes in your diet or physical activity regime.

Using This Journal

This journal has been designed to support your dieting activities. It is easy to fill and we hope it can be a source of motivation throughout your journey.

Goals / My Plan

Define your nutrition and weight loss goals as well as your exercise goals at the beginning of your journey and discuss how you plan to achieve them. Try to be as specific as you can with dates and clearly defined objectives. Establish the main rules of your diet so you have them close by.

Measurement Log

You can fill your measurements on the first day of your diet and on the last day to know how many inches or cm you are losing on the different body areas. Make sure to take the measures in a consistent way. You can also log in a few times during your journey.

Weight Loss Log

Use the Weight Loss Log to track your progress. This is an motivating way to map your progress as you gradually work toward and achieve your weight loss goals. We suggest registering your weight once a week, at the same time and dressed the same way.

Using the Journal's Pages

Jot down the date. Record the food and beverages you consume for the day. You can also, if desired, note their nutritional values (calories, protein, carbs, fat). Using the Food and Beverage Nutrition Facts tables at the end of the journal. Make sure you are within your daily calorie allotment and ensure that you are getting enough fluids and nutrients.

Record your physical activities in the Exercise section including the duration and the calories burned.

There is also a Notes section to jot down any comments, reminders, feelings, day's wins, ... you might find noteworthy of recording for that day.

References

We included several reference tools to guide your dieting journey.

You can consult the Estimated Calorie Needs per Day table to give you an idea of the number of daily calories you need according to your level of activity. If you are dieting, we do not recommend a food and beverage intake lower than 1200 calories per day for women and 1500 calories for men.

The Daily Nutritional Goals Based on Dietary Reference Intakes Recommendation table provides general guidelines for the daily food intake of protein, carbohydrate, fat, and other macronutrients, minerals, and vitamins according to age and sex groups for a balanced diet.

Food and Beverage Nutrition Facts tables will help you quickly find nutrition facts of the foods and beverages you consume.

Calories Burned in 1 Hour for Different Physical Activities table will help you figure out how much calories you can burn according to different physical activities you do for 1 hour.

There are some useful tips for successful dieting you can consult at the end of the journal.

Your physician should always be consulted to discuss any changes in your diet or physical activity regime.

Goals

_____

_____

_____

_____

_____

_____

_____

_____

_____

_____

_____

_____

_____

_____

_____

_____

_____

_____

_____

_____

_____

_____

_____

_____

_____

_____

My Plan

Measurement Log

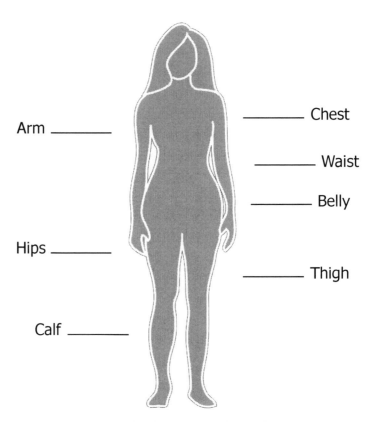

Arm

Chest

Waist

Belly

Hips

Thigh

Calf

	Start	Date	Date	Finish
Arm				
Chest				
Waist				
Belly				
Hips				
Thigh				
Calf				

Weight Loss Log

	Weight	Loss/ Gain	Cumulative Weight Loss
Day 1			
Day 2			
Day 3			
Day 4			
Day 5			
Day 6			
Day 7			
Day 8			
Day 9			
Day 10			
Day 11			
Day 12			
Day 13			
Day 14			
Day 15			
Day 16			
Day 17			
Day 18			
Day 19			
Day 20			
Day 21			
Day 22			
Day 23			
Day 24			
Day 25			
Day 26			
Day 27			
Day 28			
Day 29			
Day 30			
Day 31			
Day 32			
Day 33			
Day 34			
Day 35			
Day 36			
Day 37			
Day 38			
Day 39			
Day 40			
Day 41			
Day 42			
Day 43			
Day 44			
Day 45			

	Weight	Loss/ Gain	Cumulative Weight Loss
Day 46			
Day 47			
Day 48			
Day 49			
Day 50			
Day 51			
Day 52			
Day 53			
Day 54			
Day 55			
Day 56			
Day 57			
Day 58			
Day 59			
Day 60			
Day 61			
Day 62			
Day 63			
Day 64			
Day 65			
Day 66			
Day 67			
Day 68			
Day 69			
Day 70			
Day 71			
Day 72			
Day 73			
Day 74			
Day 75			
Day 76			
Day 77			
Day 78			
Day 79			
Day 80			
Day 81			
Day 82			
Day 83			
Day 84			
Day 85			
Day 86			
Day 87			
Day 88			
Day 89			
Day 90			

Day 1

Mo Tu We Th Fr Sa Su
_____

	Amount	Protein	Carbs	Fat	Calories
Breakfast					
Snack					
Lunch					
Snack					
Dinner					
Total					

Glasses of Water: 🥛 🥛 🥛 🥛 🥛 🥛 🥛 🥛

Servings of Fruits/Veggies :

Exercise	Duration	Calories Burned

Are you happy with how you ate and exercised today?

Food	Exercise
☹ 😐 ☺	☹ 😐 ☺

Notes _____

_____

_____

10

Day 2

_____

	Amount	Protein	Carbs	Fat	Calories
Breakfast					
Snack					
Lunch					
Snack					
Dinner					
Total					

Glasses of Water: ▯ ▯ ▯ ▯ ▯ ▯ ▯ ▯

Servings of Fruits/Veggies :

Exercise	Duration	Calories Burned

Are you happy with how you ate and exercised today?

Food	Exercise
☹ 😐 ☺	☹ 😐 ☺

Notes _____
_____
_____

Day 3

Mo Tu We Th Fr Sa Su

_____

	Amount	Protein	Carbs	Fat	Calories
Breakfast					
Snack					
Lunch					
Snack					
Dinner					
Total					

Glasses of Water: 🥛🥛🥛🥛 🥛🥛🥛🥛

Servings of Fruits/Veggies :

Exercise	Duration	Calories Burned

Are you happy with how you ate and exercised today?

Food	Exercise
☹ 😐 ☺	☹ 😐 ☺

Notes _____

_____

_____

12

Day 4

	Amount	Protein	Carbs	Fat	Calories
Breakfast					
Snack					
Lunch					
Snack					
Dinner					
Total					

Glasses of Water:

Servings of Fruits/Veggies :

Exercise	Duration	Calories Burned

Are you happy with how you ate and exercised today?

Food	Exercise
☹ 😐 ☺	☹ 😐 ☺

Notes

Day 5

_____

	Amount	Protein	Carbs	Fat	Calories
Breakfast					
Snack					
Lunch					
Snack					
Dinner					
Total					

Glasses of Water: 🥛 🥛 🥛 🥛 🥛 🥛 🥛 🥛

Servings of Fruits/Veggies :

Exercise	Duration	Calories Burned

Are you happy with how you ate and exercised today?

Food	Exercise
☹ 😐 ☺	☹ 😐 ☺

Notes _____

_____

_____

Day 6

Mo Tu We Th Fr Sa Su
_____

	Amount	Protein	Carbs	Fat	Calories
Breakfast					
Snack					
Lunch					
Snack					
Dinner					
Total					

Glasses of Water:

Servings of Fruits/Veggies :

Exercise	Duration	Calories Burned

Are you happy with how you ate and exercised today?

Food	Exercise
☹ 😐 ☺	☹ 😐 ☺

Notes

Day 7

_____

	Amount	Protein	Carbs	Fat	Calories
Breakfast					
Snack					
Lunch					
Snack					
Dinner					
Total					

Glasses of Water:

Servings of Fruits/Veggies :

Exercise	Duration	Calories Burned

Are you happy with how you ate and exercised today?

Food	Exercise
☹ 😐 ☺	☹ 😐 ☺

Notes _____

_____

_____

16

Day 8

Mo Tu We Th Fr Sa Su
_____

	Amount	Protein	Carbs	Fat	Calories
Breakfast					
Snack					
Lunch					
Snack					
Dinner					
Total					

Glasses of Water:

Servings of Fruits/Veggies :

Exercise	Duration	Calories Burned

Are you happy with how you ate and exercised today?

Food	Exercise
☹ ☺ ☺	☹ ☺ ☺

Notes _____

_____

_____

17

Day 9

Mo Tu We Th Fr Sa Su

_____

	Amount	Protein	Carbs	Fat	Calories
Breakfast					
Snack					
Lunch					
Snack					
Dinner					
Total					

Glasses of Water: 🥛 🥛 🥛 🥛 🥛 🥛 🥛 🥛

Servings of Fruits/Veggies :

Exercise	Duration	Calories Burned

Are you happy with how you ate and exercised today?

Food	Exercise
☹ 😐 ☺	☹ 😐 ☺

Notes _____

_____

_____

18

Day 10

_____

	Amount	Protein	Carbs	Fat	Calories
Breakfast					
Snack					
Lunch					
Snack					
Dinner					
Total					

Glasses of Water:

Servings of Fruits/Veggies :

Exercise	Duration	Calories Burned

Are you happy with how you ate and exercised today?

Food	Exercise
☹ ☺ ☺	☹ ☺ ☺

Notes _____

_____

Day 11

	Amount	Protein	Carbs	Fat	Calories
Breakfast					
Snack					
Lunch					
Snack					
Dinner					
Total					

Glasses of Water: ▢ ▢ ▢ ▢ ▢ ▢ ▢ ▢

Servings of Fruits/Veggies :

Exercise	Duration	Calories Burned

Are you happy with how you ate and exercised today?

Food	Exercise
☹ ☺ ☺	☹ ☺ ☺

Notes _____

_____

_____

Day 12

Mo Tu We Th Fr Sa Su
_____

	Amount	Protein	Carbs	Fat	Calories
Breakfast					
Snack					
Lunch					
Snack					
Dinner					
Total					

Glasses of Water:

Servings of Fruits/Veggies :

Exercise	Duration	Calories Burned

Are you happy with how you ate and exercised today?

Food	Exercise
☹ ☺ ☺	☹ ☺ ☺

Notes

Day 13

Mo Tu We Th Fr Sa Su
_____

	Amount	Protein	Carbs	Fat	Calories
Breakfast					
Snack					
Lunch					
Snack					
Dinner					
Total					

Glasses of Water: 🥛🥛🥛🥛 🥛🥛🥛🥛

Servings of Fruits/Veggies :

Exercise	Duration	Calories Burned

Are you happy with how you ate and exercised today?	
Food	Exercise
☹ 😐 ☺	☹ 😐 ☺

Notes _____
_____
_____

22

Day 14

Mo Tu We Th Fr Sa Su
_____

	Amount	Protein	Carbs	Fat	Calories
Breakfast					
Snack					
Lunch					
Snack					
Dinner					
Total					

Glasses of Water: ▯ ▯ ▯ ▯ ▯ ▯ ▯ ▯

Servings of Fruits/Veggies :

Exercise	Duration	Calories Burned

Are you happy with how you ate and exercised today?

Food	Exercise
☹ 😐 ☺	☹ 😐 ☺

Notes
_____
_____
_____

Day 15

Mo Tu We Th Fr Sa Su

	Amount	Protein	Carbs	Fat	Calories
Breakfast					
Snack					
Lunch					
Snack					
Dinner					
Total					

Glasses of Water:

Servings of Fruits/Veggies :

Exercise	Duration	Calories Burned

Are you happy with how you ate and exercised today?

Food	Exercise
☹ 😐 ☺	☹ 😐 ☺

Notes

Day 16

_____

	Amount	Protein	Carbs	Fat	Calories
Breakfast					
Snack					
Lunch					
Snack					
Dinner					
Total					

Glasses of Water:

Servings of Fruits/Veggies :

Exercise	Duration	Calories Burned

Are you happy with how you ate and exercised today?

Food	Exercise
☹ 😐 ☺	☹ 😐 ☺

Notes _____

_____

_____

25

Day 17

_____

	Amount	Protein	Carbs	Fat	Calories
Breakfast					
Snack					
Lunch					
Snack					
Dinner					
Total					

Glasses of Water: ▯ ▯ ▯ ▯ ▯ ▯ ▯ ▯

Servings of Fruits/Veggies :

Exercise	Duration	Calories Burned

Are you happy with how you ate and exercised today?	
Food	Exercise
☹ 😐 ☺	☹ 😐 ☺

Notes _____

_____

_____

Day 18

Mo Tu We Th Fr Sa Su

_____

	Amount	Protein	Carbs	Fat	Calories
Breakfast					
Snack					
Lunch					
Snack					
Dinner					
Total					

Glasses of Water:

Servings of Fruits/Veggies :

Exercise	Duration	Calories Burned

Are you happy with how you ate and exercised today?

Food	Exercise
☹ ☺ ☺	☹ ☺ ☺

Notes _____

_____

Day 19

	Amount	Protein	Carbs	Fat	Calories
Breakfast					
Snack					
Lunch					
Snack					
Dinner					
Total					

Glasses of Water: 🥛🥛🥛🥛 🥛🥛🥛🥛

Servings of Fruits/Veggies :

Exercise	Duration	Calories Burned

Are you happy with how you ate and exercised today?

Food	Exercise
☹ 😐 ☺	☹ 😐 ☺

Notes _____

_____

_____

Day 20

_____

	Amount	Protein	Carbs	Fat	Calories
Breakfast					
Snack					
Lunch					
Snack					
Dinner					
Total					

Glasses of Water:

Servings of Fruits/Veggies :

Exercise	Duration	Calories Burned

Are you happy with how you ate and exercised today?

Food	Exercise
☹ 😐 ☺	☹ 😐 ☺

Notes _____

_____

_____

Day 21

	Amount	Protein	Carbs	Fat	Calories
Breakfast					
Snack					
Lunch					
Snack					
Dinner					
Total					

Glasses of Water: ☐ ☐ ☐ ☐ ☐ ☐ ☐ ☐

Servings of Fruits/Veggies :

Exercise	Duration	Calories Burned

Are you happy with how you ate and exercised today?

Food	Exercise
☹ 😐 ☺	☹ 😐 ☺

Notes _____

_____

Day 22

_____

	Amount	Protein	Carbs	Fat	Calories
Breakfast					
Snack					
Lunch					
Snack					
Dinner					
Total					

Glasses of Water:

Servings of Fruits/Veggies :

Exercise	Duration	Calories Burned

Are you happy with how you ate and exercised today?

Food	Exercise
☹ 😐 ☺	☹ 😐 ☺

Notes _____

_____

_____

Day 23

	Amount	Protein	Carbs	Fat	Calories
Breakfast					
Snack					
Lunch					
Snack					
Dinner					
Total					

Glasses of Water: 🥛 🥛 🥛 🥛 🥛 🥛 🥛 🥛

Servings of Fruits/Veggies :

Exercise	Duration	Calories Burned

Are you happy with how you ate and exercised today?

Food	Exercise
☹ 😐 ☺	☹ 😐 ☺

Notes _____

Day 24

Mo Tu We Th Fr Sa Su
_____

	Amount	Protein	Carbs	Fat	Calories
Breakfast					
Snack					
Lunch					
Snack					
Dinner					
Total					

Glasses of Water:

Servings of Fruits/Veggies :

Exercise	Duration	Calories Burned

Are you happy with how you ate and exercised today?

Food	Exercise
☹ 😐 ☺	☹ 😐 ☺

Notes
_____

_____

_____

Day 25

Mo Tu We Th Fr Sa Su

_____

	Amount	Protein	Carbs	Fat	Calories
Breakfast					
Snack					
Lunch					
Snack					
Dinner					
Total					

Glasses of Water:

Servings of Fruits/Veggies :

Exercise	Duration	Calories Burned

Are you happy with how you ate and exercised today?	
Food	Exercise
☹ ☺ ☺	☹ ☺ ☺

Notes _____

_____

_____

Day 26

Mo Tu We Th Fr Sa Su
_____

	Amount	Protein	Carbs	Fat	Calories
Breakfast					
Snack					
Lunch					
Snack					
Dinner					
Total					

Glasses of Water:

Servings of Fruits/Veggies :

Exercise	Duration	Calories Burned

Are you happy with how you ate and exercised today?

Food	Exercise
☹ ☺ ☺	☹ ☺ ☺

Notes

Day 27

	Amount	Protein	Carbs	Fat	Calories
Breakfast					
Snack					
Lunch					
Snack					
Dinner					
Total					

Glasses of Water:

Servings of Fruits/Veggies :

Exercise	Duration	Calories Burned

Are you happy with how you ate and exercised today?

Food	Exercise
☹ ☺ ☺	☹ ☺ ☺

Notes

Day 28

_____

	Amount	Protein	Carbs	Fat	Calories
Breakfast					
Snack					
Lunch					
Snack					
Dinner					
Total					

Glasses of Water:

Servings of Fruits/Veggies :

Exercise	Duration	Calories Burned

Are you happy with how you ate and exercised today?

Food	Exercise
☹ ☺ ☺	☹ ☺ ☺

Notes _____

_____

_____

Day 29

	Amount	Protein	Carbs	Fat	Calories
Breakfast					
Snack					
Lunch					
Snack					
Dinner					
Total					

Glasses of Water: ▢ ▢ ▢ ▢ ▢ ▢ ▢ ▢

Servings of Fruits/Veggies :

Exercise	Duration	Calories Burned

Are you happy with how you ate and exercised today?

Food	Exercise
☹ 😐 ☺	☹ 😐 ☺

Notes _____

_____

_____

Day 30

_____

	Amount	Protein	Carbs	Fat	Calories
Breakfast					
Snack					
Lunch					
Snack					
Dinner					
Total					

Glasses of Water:

Servings of Fruits/Veggies :

Exercise	Duration	Calories Burned

Are you happy with how you ate and exercised today?

Food	Exercise
☹ 😐 ☺	☹ 😐 ☺

Notes

_____

_____

_____

Day 31

Mo Tu We Th Fr Sa Su
_____

	Amount	Protein	Carbs	Fat	Calories
Breakfast					
Snack					
Lunch					
Snack					
Dinner					
Total					

Glasses of Water: ☐ ☐ ☐ ☐ ☐ ☐ ☐ ☐   Servings of Fruits/Veggies :

Exercise	Duration	Calories Burned

Are you happy with how you ate and exercised today?

Food	Exercise
☹ 😐 ☺	☹ 😐 ☺

Notes _____

_____

Day 32

Mo Tu We Th Fr Sa Su

_____

	Amount	Protein	Carbs	Fat	Calories
Breakfast					
Snack					
Lunch					
Snack					
Dinner					
Total					

Glasses of Water:

Servings of Fruits/Veggies :

Exercise	Duration	Calories Burned

Are you happy with how you ate and exercised today?

Food	Exercise
☹ ☺ ☺	☹ ☺ ☺

Notes

_____

Day 33

Mo Tu We Th Fr Sa Su

_____

	Amount	Protein	Carbs	Fat	Calories
Breakfast					
Snack					
Lunch					
Snack					
Dinner					
Total					

Glasses of Water: 🥛 🥛 🥛 🥛 🥛 🥛 🥛

Servings of Fruits/Veggies :

Exercise	Duration	Calories Burned

Are you happy with how you ate and exercised today?

Food	Exercise
☹ 😐 ☺	☹ 😐 ☺

Notes _____

_____

_____

42

Day 34

Mo Tu We Th Fr Sa Su
_____

	Amount	Protein	Carbs	Fat	Calories
Breakfast					
Snack					
Lunch					
Snack					
Dinner					
Total					

Glasses of Water: ▢ ▢ ▢ ▢ ▢ ▢ ▢ ▢

Servings of Fruits/Veggies :

Exercise	Duration	Calories Burned

Are you happy with how you ate and exercised today?

Food	Exercise
☹ 😐 ☺	☹ 😐 ☺

Notes
_____
_____
_____

43

Day 35

Mo Tu We Th Fr Sa Su

_____

	Amount	Protein	Carbs	Fat	Calories
Breakfast					
Snack					
Lunch					
Snack					
Dinner					
Total					

Glasses of Water: 🥛🥛🥛🥛 🥛🥛🥛🥛

Servings of Fruits/Veggies :

Exercise	Duration	Calories Burned

Are you happy with how you ate and exercised today?

Food	Exercise
☹ 😐 ☺	☹ 😐 ☺

Notes _____

_____

_____

Day 36

_____

	Amount	Protein	Carbs	Fat	Calories
Breakfast					
Snack					
Lunch					
Snack					
Dinner					
Total					

Glasses of Water:

Servings of Fruits/Veggies :

Exercise	Duration	Calories Burned

Are you happy with how you ate and exercised today?

Food	Exercise
☹ ☺ ☺	☹ ☺ ☺

Notes

_____

_____

_____

Day 37

	Amount	Protein	Carbs	Fat	Calories
Breakfast					
Snack					
Lunch					
Snack					
Dinner					
Total					

Glasses of Water:

Servings of Fruits/Veggies :

Exercise	Duration	Calories Burned

Are you happy with how you ate and exercised today?

Food	Exercise
☹ 😐 ☺	☹ 😐 ☺

Notes

Day 38

_____

	Amount	Protein	Carbs	Fat	Calories
Breakfast					
Snack					
Lunch					
Snack					
Dinner					
Total					

Glasses of Water:

Servings of Fruits/Veggies :

Exercise	Duration	Calories Burned

Are you happy with how you ate and exercised today?

Food	Exercise
☹ 😐 ☺	☹ 😐 ☺

Notes _____

_____

_____

Day 39

	Amount	Protein	Carbs	Fat	Calories
Breakfast					
Snack					
Lunch					
Snack					
Dinner					
Total					

Glasses of Water:

Servings of Fruits/Veggies :

Exercise	Duration	Calories Burned

Are you happy with how you ate and exercised today?

Food	Exercise
☹ 😐 ☺	☹ 😐 ☺

Notes _____

_____

_____

Day 40

Mo Tu We Th Fr Sa Su

_____

	Amount	Protein	Carbs	Fat	Calories
Breakfast					
Snack					
Lunch					
Snack					
Dinner					
Total					

Glasses of Water:

Servings of Fruits/Veggies :

Exercise	Duration	Calories Burned

Are you happy with how you ate and exercised today?

Food	Exercise
☹ 😐 ☺	☹ 😐 ☺

Notes _____

_____

_____

Day 41

Mo Tu We Th Fr Sa Su

_____

	Amount	Protein	Carbs	Fat	Calories
Breakfast					
Snack					
Lunch					
Snack					
Dinner					
Total					

Glasses of Water: 🥛🥛🥛🥛 🥛🥛🥛🥛

Servings of Fruits/Veggies :

Exercise	Duration	Calories Burned

Are you happy with how you ate and exercised today?

Food	Exercise
☹ 😐 ☺	☹ 😐 ☺

Notes _____

_____

_____

Day 42

Mo Tu We Th Fr Sa Su

_____

	Amount	Protein	Carbs	Fat	Calories
Breakfast					
Snack					
Lunch					
Snack					
Dinner					
Total					

Glasses of Water: 🥛🥛🥛🥛 🥛🥛🥛🥛

Servings of Fruits/Veggies :

Exercise	Duration	Calories Burned

Are you happy with how you ate and exercised today?

Food	Exercise
☹ 😐 ☺	☹ 😐 ☺

Notes

_____

Day 43

	Amount	Protein	Carbs	Fat	Calories
Breakfast					
Snack					
Lunch					
Snack					
Dinner					
Total					

Glasses of Water: ▢ ▢ ▢ ▢ ▢ ▢ ▢ ▢

Servings of Fruits/Veggies :

Exercise	Duration	Calories Burned

Are you happy with how you ate and exercised today?

Food	Exercise
☹ 😐 ☺	☹ 😐 ☺

Notes

Day 44

_____

	Amount	Protein	Carbs	Fat	Calories
Breakfast					
Snack					
Lunch					
Snack					
Dinner					
Total					

Glasses of Water:

Servings of Fruits/Veggies :

Exercise	Duration	Calories Burned

Are you happy with how you ate and exercised today?

Food	Exercise
☹ 😐 ☺	☹ 😐 ☺

Notes _____

_____

_____

Day 45

	Amount	Protein	Carbs	Fat	Calories
Breakfast					
Snack					
Lunch					
Snack					
Dinner					
Total					

Glasses of Water:

Servings of Fruits/Veggies :

Exercise	Duration	Calories Burned

Are you happy with how you ate and exercised today?

Food	Exercise
☹ ☺ ☺	☹ ☺ ☺

Notes

Day 46

	Amount	Protein	Carbs	Fat	Calories
Breakfast					
Snack					
Lunch					
Snack					
Dinner					
Total					

Glasses of Water:

Servings of Fruits/Veggies :

Exercise	Duration	Calories Burned

Are you happy with how you ate and exercised today?

Food	Exercise
☹ 😐 ☺	☹ 😐 ☺

Notes

Day 47

_____

	Amount	Protein	Carbs	Fat	Calories
Breakfast					
Snack					
Lunch					
Snack					
Dinner					
Total					

Glasses of Water: ▯ ▯ ▯ ▯ ▯ ▯ ▯ ▯

Servings of Fruits/Veggies :

Exercise	Duration	Calories Burned

Are you happy with how you ate and exercised today?

Food	Exercise
☹ 😐 ☺	☹ 😐 ☺

Notes _____

_____

_____

Day 48

_____

	Amount	Protein	Carbs	Fat	Calories
Breakfast					
Snack					
Lunch					
Snack					
Dinner					
Total					

Glasses of Water:

Servings of Fruits/Veggies :

Exercise	Duration	Calories Burned

Are you happy with how you ate and exercised today?

Food	Exercise
☹ 😐 ☺	☹ 😐 ☺

Notes _____

_____

_____

Day 49

_____

	Amount	Protein	Carbs	Fat	Calories
Breakfast					
Snack					
Lunch					
Snack					
Dinner					
Total					

Glasses of Water:

Servings of Fruits/Veggies :

Exercise	Duration	Calories Burned

Are you happy with how you ate and exercised today?

Food	Exercise
☹ 😐 ☺	☹ 😐 ☺

Notes _____

_____

_____

Day 50

_____

	Amount	Protein	Carbs	Fat	Calories
Breakfast					
Snack					
Lunch					
Snack					
Dinner					
Total					

Glasses of Water:

Servings of Fruits/Veggies :

Exercise	Duration	Calories Burned

Are you happy with how you ate and exercised today?

Food	Exercise
☹ 😐 ☺	☹ 😐 ☺

Notes
_____
_____
_____

Day 51

	Amount	Protein	Carbs	Fat	Calories
Breakfast					
Snack					
Lunch					
Snack					
Dinner					
Total					

Glasses of Water: 🥛🥛🥛🥛 🥛🥛🥛🥛

Servings of Fruits/Veggies :

Exercise	Duration	Calories Burned

Are you happy with how you ate and exercised today?

Food	Exercise
☹ 😐 ☺	☹ 😐 ☺

Notes _____

_____

Day 52

	Amount	Protein	Carbs	Fat	Calories
Breakfast					
Snack					
Lunch					
Snack					
Dinner					
Total					

Glasses of Water:

Servings of Fruits/Veggies :

Exercise	Duration	Calories Burned

Are you happy with how you ate and exercised today?

Food	Exercise
☹ ☺ ☺	☹ ☺ ☺

Notes

Day 53

Mo Tu We Th Fr Sa Su

_____

	Amount	Protein	Carbs	Fat	Calories
Breakfast					
Snack					
Lunch					
Snack					
Dinner					
Total					

Glasses of Water:

Servings of Fruits/Veggies :

Exercise	Duration	Calories Burned

Are you happy with how you ate and exercised today?

Food	Exercise
☹ 😐 ☺	☹ 😐 ☺

Notes _____

_____

Day 54

	Amount	Protein	Carbs	Fat	Calories
Breakfast					
Snack					
Lunch					
Snack					
Dinner					
Total					

Glasses of Water:

Servings of Fruits/Veggies :

Exercise	Duration	Calories Burned

Are you happy with how you ate and exercised today?

Food	Exercise
☹ 😐 ☺	☹ 😐 ☺

Notes

Day 55

	Amount	Protein	Carbs	Fat	Calories
Breakfast					
Snack					
Lunch					
Snack					
Dinner					
Total					

Glasses of Water:

Servings of Fruits/Veggies :

Exercise	Duration	Calories Burned

Are you happy with how you ate and exercised today?

Food	Exercise
☹ 😐 ☺	☹ 😐 ☺

Notes

Day 56

	Amount	Protein	Carbs	Fat	Calories
Breakfast					
Snack					
Lunch					
Snack					
Dinner					
Total					

Glasses of Water:

Servings of Fruits/Veggies :

Exercise	Duration	Calories Burned

Are you happy with how you ate and exercised today?

Food	Exercise
☹ ☺ ☺	☹ ☺ ☺

Notes

Day 57

	Amount	Protein	Carbs	Fat	Calories
Breakfast					
Snack					
Lunch					
Snack					
Dinner					
Total					

Glasses of Water: 🥛🥛🥛🥛 🥛🥛🥛🥛

Servings of Fruits/Veggies :

Exercise	Duration	Calories Burned

Are you happy with how you ate and exercised today?

Food	Exercise
☹ 😐 ☺	☹ 😐 ☺

Notes _____

_____

Day 58

	Amount	Protein	Carbs	Fat	Calories
Breakfast					
Snack					
Lunch					
Snack					
Dinner					
Total					

Glasses of Water: 🥛 🥛 🥛 🥛 🥛 🥛 🥛 🥛

Servings of Fruits/Veggies :

Exercise	Duration	Calories Burned

Are you happy with how you ate and exercised today?

Food	Exercise
☹ 😐 ☺	☹ 😐 ☺

Notes

Day 59

Mo Tu We Th Fr Sa Su
_____

	Amount	Protein	Carbs	Fat	Calories
Breakfast					
Snack					
Lunch					
Snack					
Dinner					
Total					

Glasses of Water:

Servings of Fruits/Veggies :

Exercise	Duration	Calories Burned

Are you happy with how you ate and exercised today?

Food	Exercise
☹ 😐 ☺	☹ 😐 ☺

Notes

Day 60

Mo Tu We Th Fr Sa Su
_____

	Amount	Protein	Carbs	Fat	Calories
Breakfast					
Snack					
Lunch					
Snack					
Dinner					
Total					

Glasses of Water: 🥛🥛🥛🥛 🥛🥛🥛🥛

Servings of Fruits/Veggies :

Exercise	Duration	Calories Burned

Are you happy with how you ate and exercised today?

Food	Exercise
☹ 😐 ☺	☹ 😐 ☺

Notes _____
_____

69

Day 61

Mo Tu We Th Fr Sa Su
_____

	Amount	Protein	Carbs	Fat	Calories
Breakfast					
Snack					
Lunch					
Snack					
Dinner					
Total					

Glasses of Water:

Servings of Fruits/Veggies :

Exercise	Duration	Calories Burned

Are you happy with how you ate and exercised today?

Food	Exercise
☹ 😐 ☺	☹ 😐 ☺

Notes _____

_____

_____

70

Day 62

	Amount	Protein	Carbs	Fat	Calories
Breakfast					
Snack					
Lunch					
Snack					
Dinner					
Total					

Glasses of Water: 🥛🥛🥛🥛 🥛🥛🥛🥛

Servings of Fruits/Veggies :

Exercise	Duration	Calories Burned

Are you happy with how you ate and exercised today?

Food	Exercise
☹ 😐 ☺	☹ 😐 ☺

Notes _____

_____

_____

71

Day 63

Mo Tu We Th Fr Sa Su
_____

	Amount	Protein	Carbs	Fat	Calories
Breakfast					
Snack					
Lunch					
Snack					
Dinner					
Total					

Glasses of Water: ⬜ ⬜ ⬜ ⬜ ⬜ ⬜ ⬜ ⬜

Servings of Fruits/Veggies :

Exercise	Duration	Calories Burned

Are you happy with how you ate and exercised today?

Food	Exercise
☹ 😐 ☺	☹ 😐 ☺

Notes _____

_____

Day 64

_____

	Amount	Protein	Carbs	Fat	Calories
Breakfast					
Snack					
Lunch					
Snack					
Dinner					
Total					

Glasses of Water:

Servings of Fruits/Veggies :

Exercise	Duration	Calories Burned

Are you happy with how you ate and exercised today?

Food	Exercise
☹ 😐 ☺	☹ 😐 ☺

Notes _____

_____

_____

Day 65

_____

	Amount	Protein	Carbs	Fat	Calories
Breakfast					
Snack					
Lunch					
Snack					
Dinner					
Total					

Glasses of Water:

Servings of Fruits/Veggies :

Exercise	Duration	Calories Burned

Are you happy with how you ate and exercised today?

Food	Exercise
☹ 😐 ☺	☹ 😐 ☺

Notes _____

_____

_____

Day 66

	Amount	Protein	Carbs	Fat	Calories
Breakfast					
Snack					
Lunch					
Snack					
Dinner					
Total					

Glasses of Water:

Servings of Fruits/Veggies :

Exercise	Duration	Calories Burned

Are you happy with how you ate and exercised today?

Food	Exercise
☹ 😐 ☺	☹ 😐 ☺

Notes _____

_____

Day 67

	Amount	Protein	Carbs	Fat	Calories
Breakfast					
Snack					
Lunch					
Snack					
Dinner					
Total					

Glasses of Water: 🥤 🥤 🥤 🥤 🥤 🥤 🥤 🥤

Servings of Fruits/Veggies :

Exercise	Duration	Calories Burned

Are you happy with how you ate and exercised today?

Food	Exercise
☹ 😐 ☺	☹ 😐 ☺

Notes

Day 68

_____

	Amount	Protein	Carbs	Fat	Calories
Breakfast					
Snack					
Lunch					
Snack					
Dinner					
Total					

Glasses of Water:

Servings of Fruits/Veggies :

Exercise	Duration	Calories Burned

Are you happy with how you ate and exercised today?

Food	Exercise
☹ 😐 ☺	☹ 😐 ☺

Notes _____

_____

Day 69

	Amount	Protein	Carbs	Fat	Calories
Breakfast					
Snack					
Lunch					
Snack					
Dinner					
Total					

Glasses of Water:

Servings of Fruits/Veggies :

Exercise	Duration	Calories Burned

Are you happy with how you ate and exercised today?

Food	Exercise
☹ 😐 ☺	☹ 😐 ☺

Notes _____

_____

_____

Day 70

_____

	Amount	Protein	Carbs	Fat	Calories
Breakfast					
Snack					
Lunch					
Snack					
Dinner					
Total					

Glasses of Water: ▯ ▯ ▯ ▯ ▯ ▯ ▯ ▯

Servings of Fruits/Veggies :

Exercise	Duration	Calories Burned

Are you happy with how you ate and exercised today?	
Food	Exercise
☹ 😐 ☺	☹ 😐 ☺

Notes _____

_____

_____

Day 71

Mo Tu We Th Fr Sa Su
_____

	Amount	Protein	Carbs	Fat	Calories
Breakfast					
Snack					
Lunch					
Snack					
Dinner					
Total					

Glasses of Water:

Servings of Fruits/Veggies :

Exercise	Duration	Calories Burned

Are you happy with how you ate and exercised today?

Food	Exercise
☹ 😐 ☺	☹ 😐 ☺

Notes _____

_____

_____

Day 72

Mo Tu We Th Fr Sa Su

	Amount	Protein	Carbs	Fat	Calories
Breakfast					
Snack					
Lunch					
Snack					
Dinner					
Total					

Glasses of Water: 🥛🥛🥛🥛 🥛🥛🥛🥛

Servings of Fruits/Veggies :

Exercise	Duration	Calories Burned

Are you happy with how you ate and exercised today?

Food	Exercise
☹ 😐 ☺	☹ 😐 ☺

Notes

Day 73

Mo Tu We Th Fr Sa Su
_____

	Amount	Protein	Carbs	Fat	Calories
Breakfast					
Snack					
Lunch					
Snack					
Dinner					
Total					

Glasses of Water: ▢ ▢ ▢ ▢ ▢ ▢ ▢ ▢

Servings of Fruits/Veggies :

Exercise	Duration	Calories Burned

Are you happy with how you ate and exercised today?

Food	Exercise
☹ 😐 ☺	☹ 😐 ☺

Notes _____

_____

_____

Day 74

Mo Tu We Th Fr Sa Su

_____

	Amount	Protein	Carbs	Fat	Calories
Breakfast					
Snack					
Lunch					
Snack					
Dinner					
Total					

Glasses of Water:

Servings of Fruits/Veggies :

Exercise	Duration	Calories Burned

Are you happy with how you ate and exercised today?

Food	Exercise
☹ 😐 ☺	☹ 😐 ☺

Notes _____

_____

_____

Day 75

	Amount	Protein	Carbs	Fat	Calories
Breakfast					
Snack					
Lunch					
Snack					
Dinner					
Total					

Glasses of Water:

Servings of Fruits/Veggies :

Exercise	Duration	Calories Burned

Are you happy with how you ate and exercised today?

Food	Exercise
☹ 😐 ☺	☹ 😐 ☺

Notes

Day 76

_____

	Amount	Protein	Carbs	Fat	Calories
Breakfast					
Snack					
Lunch					
Snack					
Dinner					
Total					

Glasses of Water:

Servings of Fruits/Veggies :

Exercise	Duration	Calories Burned

Are you happy with how you ate and exercised today?

Food	Exercise
☹ ☺ ☺	☹ ☺ ☺

Notes _____

_____

_____

Day 77

Mo Tu We Th Fr Sa Su
_____

	Amount	Protein	Carbs	Fat	Calories
Breakfast					
Snack					
Lunch					
Snack					
Dinner					
Total					

Glasses of Water:

Servings of Fruits/Veggies :

Exercise	Duration	Calories Burned

Are you happy with how you ate and exercised today?

Food	Exercise
☹ 😐 ☺	☹ 😐 ☺

Notes _____

_____

Day 78

	Amount	Protein	Carbs	Fat	Calories
Breakfast					
Snack					
Lunch					
Snack					
Dinner					
Total					

Glasses of Water:

Servings of Fruits/Veggies :

Exercise	Duration	Calories Burned

Are you happy with how you ate and exercised today?

Food	Exercise
☹ ☺ ☺	☹ ☺ ☺

Notes _____

Day 79

Mo Tu We Th Fr Sa Su
_____

	Amount	Protein	Carbs	Fat	Calories
Breakfast					
Snack					
Lunch					
Snack					
Dinner					
Total					

Glasses of Water:

Servings of Fruits/Veggies :

Exercise	Duration	Calories Burned

Are you happy with how you ate and exercised today?

Food	Exercise
☹ 😐 ☺	☹ 😐 ☺

Notes _____

_____

_____

Day 80

	Amount	Protein	Carbs	Fat	Calories
Breakfast					
Snack					
Lunch					
Snack					
Dinner					
Total					

Glasses of Water:

Servings of Fruits/Veggies :

Exercise	Duration	Calories Burned

Are you happy with how you ate and exercised today?

Food	Exercise
☹ 😐 ☺	☹ 😐 ☺

Notes _____

_____

Day 81

Mo Tu We Th Fr Sa Su
_____

	Amount	Protein	Carbs	Fat	Calories
Breakfast					
Snack					
Lunch					
Snack					
Dinner					
Total					

Glasses of Water:

Servings of Fruits/Veggies :

Exercise	Duration	Calories Burned

Are you happy with how you ate and exercised today?

Food	Exercise
☹ 😐 ☺	☹ 😐 ☺

Notes _____

_____

_____

Day 82

_____

	Amount	Protein	Carbs	Fat	Calories
Breakfast					
Snack					
Lunch					
Snack					
Dinner					
Total					

Glasses of Water:

Servings of Fruits/Veggies :

Exercise	Duration	Calories Burned

Are you happy with how you ate and exercised today?

Food	Exercise
☹ 😐 ☺	☹ 😐 ☺

Notes _____

_____

Day 83

Mo Tu We Th Fr Sa Su
_____

	Amount	Protein	Carbs	Fat	Calories
Breakfast					
Snack					
Lunch					
Snack					
Dinner					
Total					

Glasses of Water:

Servings of Fruits/Veggies :

Exercise	Duration	Calories Burned

Are you happy with how you ate and exercised today?

Food	Exercise
☹ 😐 ☺	☹ 😐 ☺

Notes _____

92

Day 84

Mo Tu We Th Fr Sa Su

_____

	Amount	Protein	Carbs	Fat	Calories
Breakfast					
Snack					
Lunch					
Snack					
Dinner					
Total					

Glasses of Water:

Servings of Fruits/Veggies :

Exercise	Duration	Calories Burned

Are you happy with how you ate and exercised today?	
Food	Exercise
☹ 😐 ☺	☹ 😐 ☺

Notes _____

_____

_____

93

Day 85

Mo Tu We Th Fr Sa Su

_____

	Amount	Protein	Carbs	Fat	Calories
Breakfast					
Snack					
Lunch					
Snack					
Dinner					
Total					

Glasses of Water:

Servings of Fruits/Veggies :

Exercise	Duration	Calories Burned

Are you happy with how you ate and exercised today?

Food	Exercise
☹ ☺ ☺	☹ ☺ ☺

Notes _____

_____

_____

Day 86

Mo Tu We Th Fr Sa Su

_____

	Amount	Protein	Carbs	Fat	Calories
Breakfast					
Snack					
Lunch					
Snack					
Dinner					
Total					

Glasses of Water: ▯ ▯ ▯ ▯ ▯ ▯ ▯

Servings of Fruits/Veggies :

Exercise	Duration	Calories Burned

Are you happy with how you ate and exercised today?

Food	Exercise
☹ 😐 ☺	☹ 😐 ☺

Notes _____

_____

Day 87

Mo Tu We Th Fr Sa Su
_____

	Amount	Protein	Carbs	Fat	Calories
Breakfast					
Snack					
Lunch					
Snack					
Dinner					
Total					

Glasses of Water:

Servings of Fruits/Veggies :

Exercise	Duration	Calories Burned

Are you happy with how you ate and exercised today?

Food	Exercise
☹ 😐 ☺	☹ 😐 ☺

Notes
_____
_____

Day 88

	Amount	Protein	Carbs	Fat	Calories
Breakfast					
Snack					
Lunch					
Snack					
Dinner					
Total					

Glasses of Water:

Servings of Fruits/Veggies :

Exercise	Duration	Calories Burned

Are you happy with how you ate and exercised today?

Food	Exercise
☹ ☺ ☺	☹ ☺ ☺

Notes

Day 89

Mo Tu We Th Fr Sa Su

_____

	Amount	Protein	Carbs	Fat	Calories
Breakfast					
Snack					
Lunch					
Snack					
Dinner					
Total					

Glasses of Water:

Servings of Fruits/Veggies :

Exercise	Duration	Calories Burned

Are you happy with how you ate and exercised today?

Food	Exercise
☹ ☺ ☺	☹ ☺ ☺

Notes _____

_____

_____

Day 90

	Amount	Protein	Carbs	Fat	Calories
Breakfast					
Snack					
Lunch					
Snack					
Dinner					
Total					

Glasses of Water: 🥛🥛🥛🥛 🥛🥛🥛🥛

Servings of Fruits/Veggies :

Exercise	Duration	Calories Burned

Are you happy with how you ate and exercised today?

Food	Exercise
☹ 😐 ☺	☹ 😐 ☺

Notes _____

_____

_____

99

Estimated Calorie Needs per Day
by Age, Sex, and Activity Level

Gender	Age (Years)	Sedentary	Moderately Active	Active
Female	18-30	2,000	2,000-2,200	2,400
	31-50	1,800	2,000	2,200
	51+	1,600	1,800	2,000-2,200
Male	18-30	2,400	2,600-2,800	3,000
	31-50	2,200	2,400-2,600	2,800-3,000
	51+	2,000	2,200-2,400	2,400-2,800

Notes

[a] Sedentary means a lifestyle that includes only the physical activity of independent living.

[b] Moderately Active means a lifestyle that includes physical activity equivalent to walking about 1.5 to 3 miles per day at 3 to 4 miles per hour, in addition to the activities of independent living.

[c] Active means a lifestyle that includes physical activity equivalent to walking more than 3 miles per day at 3 to 4 miles per hour, in addition to the activities of independent living.

[d] Estimates for females do not include women who are pregnant or breastfeeding.

Source: Institute of Medicine. Dietary Reference Intakes for Energy, Carbohydrate, Fiber, Fat, Fatty Acids, Cholesterol, Protein, and Amino Acids. Washington (DC): The National Academies Press; 2002.

Daily Nutritional Goals
Based on Dietary Reference Intakes Recommendations

	Female 18-30	Male 18-30	Female 31-50	Male 31-50	Female 51+	Male 51+
Calorie level(s) assessed	2,000	2,400, 2,600, 3,000	1,800	2,200	1,600	2,000
Macronutrients						
Protein, g	46	56	46	56	46	56
Protein, % kcal	10-35	10-35	10-35	10-35	10-35	10-35
Carbohydrate, g	130	130	130	130	130	130
Carbohydrate, % kcal	45-65	45-65	45-65	45-65	45-65	45-65
Dietary fiber, g	28	33.6	25.2	30.8	22.4	28
Added sugars, % kcal	<10%	<10%	<10%	<10%	<10%	<10%
Total fat, % kcal	20-35	20-35	20-35	20-35	20-35	20-35
Saturated fat, % kcal	<10%	<10%	<10%	<10%	<10%	<10%
Linoleic acid, g	12	17	12	17	11	14
Linolenic acid, g	1.1	1.6	1.1	1.6	1.1	1.6
Minerals						
Calcium, mg	1,000	1,000	1,000	1,000	1,200	1,000[b]
Iron, mg	18	8	18	8	8	8
Magnesium, mg	310	400	320	420	320	420
Phosphorus, mg	700	700	700	700	700	700
Potassium, mg	4,700	4,700	4,700	4,700	4,700	4,700
Sodium, mg	2,300	2,300	2,300	2,300	2,300	2,300
Zinc, mg	8	11	8	11	8	11
Copper, mcg	900	900	900	900	900	900
Manganese, mg	1.8	2.3	1.8	2.3	1.8	2.3
Selenium, mcg	55	55	55	55	55	55
Vitamins						
Vitamin A, mg RAE	700	900	700	900	700	900
Vitamin E, mg AT	15	15	15	15	15	15
Vitamin D, IU	600	600	600	600	600c	600c
Vitamin C, mg	75	90	75	90	75	90
Thiamin, mg	1.1	1.2	1.1	1.2	1.1	1.2
Riboflavin, mg	1.1	1.3	1.1	1.3	1.1	1.3
Niacin, mg	14	16	14	16	14	16
Vitamin B6, mg	1.3	1.3	1.3	1.3	1.5	1.7
Vitamin B12, mcg	2.4	2.4	2.4	2.4	2.4	2.4
Choline, mg	425	550	425	550	425	550
Vitamin K, mcg	90	120	90	120	90	120
Folate, mcg DFE	400	400	400	400	400	400

Source: Institute of Medicine. Dietary Reference Intakes: The essential guide to nutrient requirements. Washington (DC): The National Academies Press; 2006.

Source: Institute of Medicine. Dietary Reference Intakes for Calcium and Vitamin D. Washington (DC): The National Academies Press; 2010.

Food and Beverage
Nutrition Facts

Baked Goods					
Description	**Weight (g)**	**Measure**	**Energy (kcal)**	**Protein (g)**	**Carbohydrate, by difference (g)**
ARCHWAY Home Style Cookies, Date Filled Oatmeal	25	1.0 serving	100	1.17	17.04
ARCHWAY Home Style Cookies, Iced Molasses	28	1.0 serving	118	0.98	19.35
ARCHWAY Home Style Cookies, Iced Oatmeal	28	1.0 serving	122	1.37	18.69
ARCHWAY Home Style Cookies, Molasses	26	1.0 serving	105	1.1	18.05
ARCHWAY Home Style Cookies, Raspberry Filled	25	1.0 serving	100	1.09	16.48
Artificial Blueberry Muffin Mix, dry	31	1.0 muffin	126	1.46	24.01
AUSTIN, Grilled Cheese on Wafer Crackers, sandwich-type	39	1.0 package	192	3.08	24.18
AUSTIN, Peanut Butter on Toasty Crackers, sandwich-type, reduced fat	36	1.0 package	167	3.42	24.19
Bagels, oat bran	26	1.0 mini bagel (2-1/2" dia)	66	2.78	13.86
Bagels, plain, enriched, with calcium propionate (includes onion, poppy, sesame)	99	1.0 bagel	261	10.45	51.86
Bagels, plain, enriched, with calcium propionate (includes onion, poppy, sesame), toasted	24	1.0 mini bagel (2-1/2" dia)	69	2.67	13.77
BEAR NAKED, Double Chocolate Cookies	30	1.0 cookie	127	1.98	20.07
BEAR NAKED, Fruit & Nut Cookies	30	1.0 cookie	133	2.25	18.48
Biscuits, mixed grain, refrigerated dough	28.4	1.0 oz	75	1.73	13.44
Biscuits, plain or buttermilk, dry mix	120	1.0 cup, purchased	514	9.6	76.08
Biscuits, plain or buttermilk, frozen, baked	28.4	1.0 oz	96	1.76	15.27
Biscuits, plain or buttermilk, refrigerated dough, higher fat	58	1.0 biscuit	178	3.86	26.87
Bread stuffing, bread, dry mix	28.4	1.0 oz	109	3.12	21.6
Bread stuffing, cornbread, dry mix	28.4	1.0 oz	110	2.83	21.74
Bread stuffing, cornbread, dry mix, prepared	28.4	1.0 oz	51	0.82	6.21
Bread, cheese	48	1.0 slice	196	5	21.52
Bread, cornbread, dry mix, prepared with 2% milk, 80% margarine, and eggs	51	1.0 muffin	168	3.36	27.77
Bread, cornbread, prepared from recipe, made with low fat (2%) milk	28.4	1.0 oz	75	1.9	12.33
Bread, cracked-wheat	28.4	1.0 oz	74	2.47	14.03
Bread, french or vienna, toasted (includes sourdough)	28.4	1.0 oz	90	3.69	17.56
Bread, irish soda, prepared from recipe	28.4	1.0 oz	82	1.87	15.88
Bread, oat bran	28.4	1.0 oz	67	2.95	11.28
Bread, oatmeal, toasted	28.4	1.0 oz	83	2.61	14.94
Bread, pan dulce, sweet yeast bread	63	1.0 slice (average weight of 1 slice)	231	5.93	35.52
Bread, pita, white, enriched	60	1.0 pita, large (6-1/2" dia)	165	5.46	33.42
Bread, pound cake type, pan de torta salvadoran	55	1.0 serving	214	3.88	28.21

Bread, protein (includes gluten)	28.4	1.0 oz	69	3.43	12.42
Bread, reduced-calorie, oatmeal	28.4	1.0 oz	60	2.15	12.28
Bread, reduced-calorie, wheat	28.4	1.0 oz	62	3.78	12.04
Bread, reduced-calorie, white	28.4	1.0 oz	59	2.47	12.56
Bread, rye	28.4	1.0 oz	73	2.41	13.69
Bread, salvadoran sweet cheese (quesadilla salvadorena)	55	1.0 serving (approximate serving size)	206	3.92	26.31
Bread, wheat	29	1.0 slice	79	3.09	13.79
Bread, wheat bran	28.4	1.0 oz	70	2.49	13.55
Bread, wheat germ, toasted	28.4	1.0 oz	83	3.03	15.39
Bread, white wheat	28	1.0 slice	67	2.98	12.29
Bread, white, commercially prepared, toasted	28.4	1.0 oz	82	2.55	15.45
Bread, whole-wheat, commercially prepared	32	1.0 slice	81	3.98	13.67
Cake, angelfood, commercially prepared	28	1.0 piece (1/12 of 12 oz cake)	72	1.65	16.18
Cake, angelfood, dry mix, prepared	50	1.0 piece (1/12 of 10" dia)	128	3.05	29.35
Cake, cherry fudge with chocolate frosting	28.4	1.0 oz	75	0.68	10.77
Cake, chocolate, prepared from recipe without frosting	95	1.0 piece (1/12 of 9" dia)	352	5.04	50.73
Cake, pudding-type, german chocolate, dry mix	43	1.0 serving	150	1.79	34.94
Cake, shortcake, biscuit-type, prepared from recipe	28.4	1.0 oz	98	1.73	13.75
Cake, snack cakes, creme-filled, sponge	28.4	1.0 oz	106	0.98	18.15
Cake, sponge, commercially prepared	28.4	1.0 oz	82	1.53	17.29
Cake, white, dry mix, special dietary (includes lemon-flavored)	28.4	1.0 oz	113	0.85	22.57
Cake, yellow, prepared from recipe without frosting	68	1.0 piece (1/12 of 8" dia)	245	3.6	36.04
Cheesecake commercially prepared	28.4	1.0 oz	91	1.56	7.23
Coffeecake, cinnamon with crumb topping, dry mix	28.4	1.0 oz	124	1.36	22.03
Coffeecake, cinnamon with crumb topping, dry mix, prepared	28.4	1.0 oz	90	1.56	14.97
Coffeecake, creme-filled with chocolate frosting	28.4	1.0 oz	94	1.42	15.25
CONTINENTAL MILLS, KRUSTEAZ Almond Poppyseed Muffin Mix, Artificially Flavored, dry	40	1.0 serving	167	2.24	30.24
Cookies, brownies, dry mix, sugar free	28.4	1.0 oz	121	0.82	22.79
Cookies, brownies, prepared from recipe	28.4	1.0 oz	132	1.76	14.23
Cookies, chocolate chip, commercially prepared, regular, higher fat, enriched	12.9	1.0 cookie	63	0.66	8.43
Cookies, chocolate chip, commercially prepared, regular, lower fat	34	1.0 serving 3 cookies	153	2.03	22.95
Cookies, chocolate chip, refrigerated dough	33	1.0 serving	149	1.31	20.14
Cookies, chocolate sandwich, with creme filling, regular	36	3.0 cookie	167	1.88	25.56

Cookies, chocolate sandwich, with creme filling, special dietary	28.4	1.0 oz	131	1.28	19.28
Cookies, chocolate sandwich, with extra creme filling	28.4	1.0 oz	141	1.23	19.33
Cookies, chocolate wafers	28.4	1.0 oz	123	1.87	20.61
Cookies, fig bars	28.4	1.0 oz	99	1.05	20.1
Cookies, molasses	28.4	1.0 oz	122	1.59	20.92
Cookies, oatmeal, commercially prepared, regular	28.4	1.0 oz	128	1.76	19.48
Cookies, oatmeal, commercially prepared, special dietary	28.4	1.0 oz	127	1.36	19.82
Cookies, oatmeal, prepared from recipe, with raisins	28.4	1.0 oz	123	1.84	19.39
Cookies, oatmeal, refrigerated dough	28.4	1.0 oz	120	1.53	16.75
Cookies, oatmeal, refrigerated dough, baked	28.4	1.0 oz	134	1.7	18.63
Cookies, peanut butter sandwich, regular	28.4	1.0 oz	136	2.49	18.6
Cookies, peanut butter sandwich, special dietary	28.4	1.0 oz	152	2.83	14.4
Cookies, peanut butter, commercially prepared, regular	28.4	1.0 oz	134	2.53	16.49
Cookies, peanut butter, commercially prepared, soft-type	28.4	1.0 oz	130	1.5	16.36
Cookies, shortbread, commercially prepared, pecan	28.4	1.0 oz	154	1.39	16.53
Cookies, shortbread, commercially prepared, plain	28.4	1.0 oz	146	1.52	18.08
Cookies, sugar wafer, with creme filling, sugar free	28.4	1.0 oz	151	1.01	18.78
Cookies, sugar wafers with creme filling, regular	36	3.0 cookies	181	1.38	25.43
Cookies, sugar, commercially prepared, regular (includes vanilla)	28.4	1.0 oz	132	1.52	19.09
Cookies, vanilla sandwich with creme filling	28.4	1.0 oz	137	1.28	20.44
Cracker meal	28.4	1.0 oz	109	2.64	22.94
Crackers, cheese, regular	14.2	0.5 oz	69	1.55	8.44
Crackers, cheese, sandwich-type with cheese filling	39	6.0 cracker 1 cracker = 6.5g	191	3.48	22.92
Crackers, cream, GAMESA SABROSAS	31	11.0 crackers (1 NLEA serving)	150	2.17	20.01
Crackers, melba toast, rye (includes pumpernickel)	14.2	0.5 oz	55	1.65	10.98
Crackers, rusk toast	14.2	0.5 oz	58	1.92	10.27
Crackers, rye, wafers, seasoned	14.2	0.5 oz	54	1.28	10.48
Crackers, saltines, whole wheat (includes multi-grain)	14	1.0 serving	56	1	9.55
Crackers, standard snack-type, regular	16	5.0 crackers	82	1.06	9.81
Crackers, standard snack-type, sandwich, with cheese filling	14.2	0.5 oz	68	1.32	8.76
Crackers, standard snack-type, sandwich, with peanut butter filling	14.2	0.5 oz	70	1.63	8.29
Crackers, wheat, regular	34	16.0 crackers 1 serving	155	2.48	24.05
Crackers, wheat, sandwich, with cheese filling	14.2	0.5 oz	71	1.39	8.26

Crackers, wheat, sandwich, with peanut butter filling	14.2	0.5 oz	70	1.92	7.64
Cream puff, eclair, custard or cream filled, iced	113	4.0 oz	377	4.98	42.3
Croissants, apple	28.4	1.0 oz	72	2.1	10.52
Croissants, butter	28.4	1.0 oz	115	2.32	12.98
Croissants, cheese	28.4	1.0 oz	117	2.61	13.32
Croutons, plain	14.2	0.5 oz	58	1.69	10.44
Croutons, seasoned	14.2	0.5 oz	66	1.53	9.02
Danish pastry, cheese	28.4	1.0 oz	106	2.27	10.55
Danish pastry, cinnamon, enriched	28.4	1.0 oz	114	1.98	12.64
English muffins, mixed-grain (includes granola)	28.4	1.0 oz	67	2.58	13.13
Focaccia, Italian flatbread, plain	57	1.0 piece	142	5	20.42
Garlic bread, frozen	43	1.0 slice presliced	150	3.59	17.94
GEORGE WESTON BAKERIES, Brownberry Sage and Onion Stuffing Mix, dry	67	1.0 serving	261	8.91	48.71
HEINZ, WEIGHT WATCHER, Chocolate Eclair, frozen	59	1.0 eclair, frozen	142	2.6	23.78
KASHI, H2H Woven Wheat Cracker, Roasted Garlic	30	7.0 cracker	132	3.15	21.96
KASHI, TLC, Honey Sesame Crackers	30	15.0 cracker	119	2.61	21.66
KASHI, TLC, Original 7-Grain Crackers	30	15.0 crackers	116	4.17	18.96
KEEBLER, KEEBLER Chocolate Graham SELECTS	31	1.0 serving	144	2.2	22.26
KEEBLER, Vanilla Wafers	30	8.0 cookies	139	1.2	21.93
Keikitos (muffins), Latino bakery item	42	1.0 piece	196	2.86	22.33
KELLOGG'S EGGO Lowfat Blueberry Nutri-Grain Waffles	35	1.0 waffle, round (1" dia) (include frozen)	73	2.08	14.95
KELLOGG'S, BEANATURAL, Original 3-Bean Chips	28	12.0 chips	136	6.41	13.02
KELLOGG'S, EGGO, Biscuit Scramblers, Bacon, Egg & Cheese	105	1.0 bscuit	271	9.24	40.21
KELLOGG'S, EGGO, French Toaster Sticks, Cinnamon	90	2.0 pieces	225	4.32	38.34
KELLOGG'S, EGGO, Mini Muffin Tops, Blueberry	46	1.0 set	135	2.3	21.07
KELLOGG'S, EGGO, NUTRI-GRAIN, Waffles, Low Fat	70	2.0 waffles 1 serving	141	4.55	27.3
KELLOGG'S, EGGO, Waffles, Homestyle, Low Fat	70	2.0 waffles 1 serving	160	4.41	31.43
MARTHA WHITE FOODS, Martha White's Buttermilk Biscuit Mix, dry	41	1.0 serving	159	3.2	24.36
MARTHA WHITE FOODS, Martha White's Chewy Fudge Brownie Mix, dry	28	1.0 serving	114	1.24	23.4
MCKEE BAKING, LITTLE DEBBIE NUTTY BARS, Wafers with Peanut Butter, Chocolate Covered	57	1.0 serving	312	4.56	31.46
MISSION FOODS, MISSION Flour Tortillas, Soft Taco, 8 inch	51	1.0 serving	146	4.44	25.3
Muffin, blueberry, commercially prepared, low-fat	71	1.0 muffin small	181	3	35.54

Description	Weight (g)	Measure	Energy (kcal)	Protein (g)	Carbohydrate (g)
NABISCO, NABISCO GRAHAMS Crackers	28	1.0 serving	119	1.96	21.34
NABISCO, NABISCO OREO CRUNCHIES, Cookie Crumb Topping	11	1.0 serving	52	0.53	7.73
NABISCO, NABISCO RITZ Crackers	3.3	1.0 cracker	16	0.24	2.1
Pancakes, buckwheat, dry mix, incomplete	28.4	1.0 oz	96	3.09	20.21
Pancakes, plain, frozen, ready-to-heat, microwave (includes buttermilk)	28.4	1.0 oz	68	1.67	12.28
Pie Crust, Cookie-type, Chocolate, Ready Crust	182	1.0 crust	881	11.07	117.35
Pie crust, deep dish, frozen, baked, made with enriched flour	202	1.0 pie crust (average weight)	1052	12.32	105.99
Pie crust, deep dish, frozen, unbaked, made with enriched flour	225	1.0 pie crust (average weight)	1053	12.42	105.28
Pie, banana cream, prepared from recipe	28.4	1.0 oz	76	1.25	9.33
Pie, blueberry, commercially prepared	28.4	1.0 oz	66	0.51	9.89
Pie, cherry, commercially prepared	28.4	1.0 oz	74	0.57	11.28
Pie, Dutch Apple, Commercially Prepared	131	0.125 pie 1 pie (1/8 of 9" pie)	380	2.84	58.35
Pie, fried pies, fruit	28.4	1.0 oz	90	0.85	12.08
PILLSBURY, Buttermilk Biscuits, Artificial Flavor, refrigerated dough	64	1.0 biscuit	151	4.1	30.12
PILLSBURY, Chocolate Chip Cookies, refrigerated dough	38	1.0 serving 2 cookies	171	1.45	23.09
PILLSBURY, Cinnamon Rolls with Icing, refrigerated dough	44	1.0 serving 1 roll with icing	145	1.91	23.5
PILLSBURY, Crusty French Loaf, refrigerated dough	52	1.0 serving	126	4.47	24.1
Toaster pastries, fruit, toasted (include apple, blueberry, cherry, strawberry)	51	1.0 pastry	209	2.4	37.08
Tortillas, ready-to-bake or -fry, flour, shelf stable	49	1.0 tortilla	146	3.92	24.14

Dairy and Eggs

Description	Weight (g)	Measure	Energy (kcal)	Protein (g)	Carbohydrate, by difference (g)
Butter, salted	5	1.0 pat (1" sq, 1/3" high)	36	0.04	0
Cheese food, pasteurized process, American, vitamin D fortified	113	1.0 cup	373	19.05	9.67
Cheese spread, pasteurized process, American	140	1.0 cup, diced	406	22.97	12.22
Cheese substitute, mozzarella	113	1.0 cup, shredded	280	12.96	26.75
Cheese, American, nonfat or fat free	19	1.0 serving	24	4	2
Cheese, blue	28.4	1.0 oz	100	6.07	0.66
Cheese, camembert	28.4	1.0 oz	85	5.61	0.13
Cheese, cheddar	132	1.0 cup, diced	533	30.19	4.08

Cheese, cottage, creamed, large or small curd	113	4.0 oz	111	12.57	3.82
Cheese, cottage, creamed, with fruit	113	4.0 oz	110	12.08	5.21
Cheese, cottage, lowfat, 1% milkfat	113	4.0 oz	81	14	3.07
Cheese, cottage, lowfat, 2% milkfat	113	4.0 oz	92	11.81	5.38
Cheese, cottage, nonfat, uncreamed, dry, large or small curd	145	1.0 cup (not packed)	104	14.99	9.66
Cheese, cream	14.5	1.0 tbsp	51	0.89	0.8
Cheese, feta	150	1.0 cup, crumbled	396	21.32	6.13
Cheese, mexican, queso chihuahua	132	1.0 cup, diced	494	28.46	7.34
Cheese, mozzarella, low moisture, part-skim	132	1.0 cup, diced	389	31.35	7.37
Cheese, mozzarella, whole milk	112	1.0 cup, shredded	336	24.83	2.45
Cheese, muenster	132	1.0 cup, diced	486	30.9	1.48
Cheese, neufchatel	28.4	1.0 oz	72	2.59	1.02
Cheese, parmesan, grated	100	1.0 cup	420	28.42	13.91
Cheese, pasteurized process, American, fortified with vitamin D	28.4	1.0 oz	104	5.14	1.36
Cheese, pasteurized process, swiss	140	1.0 cup, diced	468	34.62	2.94
Cheese, provolone	132	1.0 cup, diced	463	33.77	2.82
Cheese, ricotta, part skim milk	124	0.5 cup	171	14.12	6.37
Cheese, ricotta, whole milk	124	0.5 cup	216	13.96	3.77
Cheese, swiss	132	1.0 cup, diced	519	35.59	1.9
Cream substitute, liquid, with lauric acid oil and sodium caseinate	15	1.0 container, individual	20	0.15	1.71
Cream, fluid, half and half	30.2	1.0 fl oz	37	0.95	1.43
Cream, fluid, heavy whipping	120	1.0 cup, whipped	408	3.41	3.29
Cream, fluid, light (coffee cream or table cream)	30	1.0 fl oz	57	0.89	0.85
Cream, fluid, light whipping	120	1.0 cup, whipped	350	2.6	3.55
Cream, sour, cultured	12	1.0 tbsp	24	0.29	0.56
Cream, sour, reduced fat, cultured	15	1.0 tbsp	20	0.44	0.64
Cream, whipped, cream topping, pressurized	60	1.0 cup	154	1.92	7.49
Dessert topping, powdered	43	1.5 oz	248	2.11	22.59
Dessert topping, powdered, 1.5 ounce prepared with 1/2 cup milk	80	1.0 cup	155	2.89	13.7
Dessert topping, pressurized	70	1.0 cup	185	0.69	11.25
Egg substitute, powder	9.9	0.35 oz	44	5.49	2.16
Egg, white, raw, fresh	33	1.0 large	17	3.6	0.24
Egg, whole, cooked, fried	46	1.0 large	90	6.26	0.38
Egg, whole, cooked, omelet	15	1.0 tbsp	23	1.59	0.1
Egg, whole, cooked, poached	50	1.0 large	72	6.25	0.35
Egg, whole, raw, fresh	50	1.0 large	72	6.28	0.36
Egg, yolk, raw, frozen, sugared, pasteurized	28.4	1.0 oz	87	3.93	3.1
Eggnog	254	1.0 cup	224	11.56	20.45
Milk shakes, thick chocolate	28.4	1.0 fl oz	34	0.87	6.01
Milk substitutes, fluid, with lauric acid oil	244	1.0 cup	149	4.27	15.03
Milk, buttermilk, dried	30	0.25 cup	116	10.29	14.7

Milk, canned, condensed, sweetened	38.2	1.0 fl oz	123	3.02	20.78
Milk, canned, evaporated, nonfat, with added vitamin A and vitamin D	31.9	1.0 fl oz	25	2.41	3.62
Milk, canned, evaporated, with added vitamin D and without added vitamin A	31.5	1.0 fl oz	42	2.15	3.16
Milk, chocolate, fluid, commercial, reduced fat, with added vitamin A and vitamin D	250	1.0 cup	190	7.47	30.32
Milk, chocolate, fluid, commercial, whole, with added vitamin A and vitamin D	250	1.0 cup	208	7.92	25.85
Milk, dry, nonfat, calcium reduced	28.4	1.0 oz	100	10.06	14.69
Milk, dry, nonfat, regular, without added vitamin A and vitamin D	30	0.25 cup	109	10.85	15.59
Milk, lowfat, fluid, 1% milkfat, protein fortified, with added vitamin A and vitamin D	246	1.0 cup	118	9.67	13.58
Milk, nonfat, fluid, protein fortified, with added vitamin A and vitamin D (fat free and skim)	246	1.0 cup	101	9.74	13.68
Milk, producer, fluid, 3.7% milkfat	244	1.0 cup	156	8	11.35
Milk, reduced fat, fluid, 2% milkfat, protein fortified, with added vitamin A and vitamin D	246	1.0 cup	138	9.72	13.51
Milk, sheep, fluid	245	1.0 cup	265	14.65	13.13
Parmesan cheese topping, fat free	5	1.0 tablespoon	18	2	--
Sour dressing, non-butterfat, cultured, filled cream-type	12	1.0 tbsp	21	0.39	0.56
Whey, sweet, dried	145	1.0 cup	512	18.75	107.97
Yogurt, fruit, low fat, 11 grams protein per 8 ounce	170	1.0 container (6 oz)	178	8.26	31.62
Yogurt, fruit, low fat, 9 grams protein per 8 ounce	170	1.0 container (6 oz)	168	6.77	31.69
Yogurt, plain, low fat, 12 grams protein per 8 ounce	170	1.0 container (6 oz)	107	8.93	11.97
Yogurt, plain, whole milk, 8 grams protein per 8 ounce	170	1.0 container (6 oz)	104	5.9	7.92

Cereal, Grains, Pasta					
Description	Weight (g)	Measure	Energy (kcal)	Protein (g)	Carbohydrate, by difference (g)
Barley flour or meal	148	1.0 cup	511	15.54	110.29
Corn flour, yellow, masa, enriched	114	1.0 cup	414	9.64	87.31
Corn grain, white	166	1.0 cup	606	15.64	123.27
Cornmeal, white, self-rising, bolted, with wheat flour added, enriched	170	1.0 cup	592	14.3	124.83
Cornmeal, white, self-rising, degermed, enriched	138	1.0 cup	490	11.61	103.21
Cornmeal, whole-grain, white	122	1.0 cup	442	9.91	93.81
Macaroni, vegetable, enriched, cooked	134	1.0 cup spiral shaped	172	6.07	35.66
Macaroni, vegetable, enriched, dry	84	1.0 cup spiral shaped	308	11.04	62.9

Description	Weight (g)	Measure	Energy (kcal)	Protein (g)	Carbohydrate, by difference (g)
Noodles, egg, dry, unenriched	38	1.0 cup	146	5.38	27.08
Noodles, egg, spinach, enriched, cooked	160	1.0 cup	211	8.06	38.8
Noodles, egg, unenriched, cooked, without added salt	160	1.0 cup	221	7.26	40.26
Noodles, japanese, somen, cooked	176	1.0 cup	231	7.04	48.47
Noodles, japanese, somen, dry	57	2.0 oz	203	6.47	42.24
Oat flour, partially debranned	104	1.0 cup	420	15.25	68.33
Pasta, dry, enriched	91	1.0 cup spaghetti	338	11.87	67.95
Pasta, dry, unenriched	91	1.0 cup spaghetti	338	11.87	67.95
Pasta, fresh-refrigerated, plain, as purchased	128	4.5 oz	369	14.48	70.05
Pasta, fresh-refrigerated, spinach, as purchased	128	4.5 oz	370	14.41	71.32
Pasta, whole-wheat, dry	91	1.0 cup spaghetti	320	12.62	66.77
Rice flour, brown	158	1.0 cup	574	11.42	120.84
Rice noodles, cooked	176	1.0 cup	190	3.15	42.26
Rice, white, long-grain, regular, cooked, unenriched, with salt	158	1.0 cup	205	4.25	44.51
Rice, white, long-grain, regular, raw, unenriched	185	1.0 cup	675	13.19	147.91
Rice, white, medium-grain, cooked, unenriched	186	1.0 cup	242	4.43	53.18
Sorghum flour, whole-grain	121	1.0 cup	434	10.2	92.73
Teff, cooked	252	1.0 cup	255	9.75	50.05
Wheat flour, white, all-purpose, enriched, calcium-fortified	125	1.0 cup	455	12.91	95.39
Wheat flour, white, all-purpose, unenriched	125	1.0 cup	455	12.91	95.39
Wheat flour, white, bread, enriched	137	1.0 cup	495	16.41	99.37

Breakfast Cereal					
Description	Weight (g)	Measure	Energy (kcal)	Protein (g)	Carbohydrate, by difference (g)
Cereals ready-to-eat, BARBARA'S PUFFINS, original	27	0.75 cup (1 NLEA serving)	90	2	22.68
Cereals ready-to-eat, GENERAL MILLS, COCOA PUFFS, 25% Reduced Sugar	30	1.0 cup (1 NLEA serving)	114	1.95	24.81
Cereals ready-to-eat, GENERAL MILLS, FIBER ONE 80 Calories, Chocolate Squares	30	0.75 cup (1 NLEA serving)	76	0.99	25.2
Cereals ready-to-eat, GENERAL MILLS, Honey KIX	33	1.25 cup (1 NLEA serving)	120	2.11	27.39
Cereals ready-to-eat, GENERAL MILLS, LUCKY CHARMS	27	0.75 cup (1 NLEA serving)	103	2.07	21.84
Cereals ready-to-eat, GENERAL MILLS, Rice CHEX	27	1.0 cup (1 NLEA serving)	101	1.73	22.97
Cereals ready-to-eat, granola, homemade	122	1.0 cup	597	16.68	65.73
Cereals ready-to-eat, KASHI GOLEAN CRISP Cinnamon Crumble	51	0.75 cup (1 NLEA serving)	185	11.27	31.92

Food	Weight (g)	Measure	Calories	Protein	Carbohydrate
Cereals ready-to-eat, KASHI Honey Sunshine	30	0.75 cup (1 NLEA serving)	100	2.34	24.6
Cereals ready-to-eat, KELLOGG'S APPLE JACKS with marshmallows	28	1.0 cup (1 NLEA serving)	106	1.2	25.09
Cereals ready-to-eat, KELLOGG's FROSTED MINI-WHEATS Bite Size Blueberry Muffin	55	25.0 biscuits (1 NLEA serving)	194	4.73	46.64
Cereals ready-to-eat, KELLOGG'S FROSTED MINI-WHEATS Touch of Fruit in the Middle, Raspberry	55	24.0 biscuits (1 NLEA serving)	188	4.84	45.16
Cereals ready-to-eat, KELLOGG'S KRAVE double chocolate cereal	30	0.75 cup (1 NLEA serving)	119	2.13	22.77
Cereals ready-to-eat, NATURE'S PATH, Organic FLAX PLUS flakes	30	0.75 cup (1 NLEA serving)	105	3.57	22.58
Cereals ready-to-eat, POST HONEY BUNCHES OF OATS with cinnamon bunches	30	0.75 cup (1 NLEA serving)	120	2.13	24.84
Cereals ready-to-eat, POST, COCOA PEBBLES	29	0.75 cup (1 NLEA serving)	115	1.39	24.85
Cereals ready-to-eat, POST, HONEY BUNCHES OF OATS with vanilla bunches	56	1.0 cup (1 NLEA serving)	221	4.42	45.81
Cereals ready-to-eat, POST, Honeycomb Cereal	32	1.5 cup (1 NLEA serving)	126	1.92	27.72
Cereals ready-to-eat, POST, Shredded Wheat, original big biscuit	47	2.0 biscuits (1 NLEA serving)	158	5.34	37.11
Cereals ready-to-eat, POST, Shredded Wheat, original spoon-size	49	1.0 cup (1 NLEA serving)	172	5.78	39.89
Cereals ready-to-eat, QUAKER Oatmeal Squares, Golden Maple	56	1.0 cup (1 NLEA serving)	213	6.33	43.7
Cereals ready-to-eat, QUAKER, Maple Brown Sugar LIFE Cereal	32	0.75 cup (1 NLEA serving)	119	2.93	25.24
Cereals ready-to-eat, QUAKER, QUAKER CRUNCHY BRAN	27	0.75 cup (1 NLEA serving)	89	1.72	22.59
Cereals ready-to-eat, QUAKER, QUAKER OAT LIFE, plain	32	0.75 cup (1 NLEA serving)	120	3.19	24.88
Cereals ready-to-eat, QUAKER, QUAKER Puffed Wheat	15	1.0 cup (1 NLEA serving)	55	2.44	11.46
Cereals ready-to-eat, rice, puffed, fortified	14	1.0 cup	56	0.88	12.57
Cereals, corn grits, white, regular and quick, enriched, cooked with water, with salt	257	1.0 cup	182	4.39	37.93
Cereals, corn grits, white, regular and quick, enriched, cooked with water, without salt	257	1.0 cup	182	4.39	37.93
Cereals, corn grits, yellow, regular and quick, enriched, cooked with water, without salt	233	1.0 cup	151	2.87	32.29
Cereals, CREAM OF RICE, cooked with water, with salt	244	1.0 cup	127	2.2	28.06
Cereals, CREAM OF RICE, dry	45	0.25 cup (1 NLEA serving)	166	2.83	37.08

Description	Weight (g)	Measure	Energy (kcal)	Protein (g)	Carbohydrate, by difference (g)
Cereals, CREAM OF WHEAT, instant, dry	11.5	1.0 tbsp	42	1.22	8.68
Cereals, CREAM OF WHEAT, instant, prepared with water, without salt	241	1.0 cup	149	4.43	31.52
Cereals, MALT-O-MEAL, chocolate, dry	35	3.0 tbsp (1 NLEA serving)	127	3.71	27.84
Cereals, oats, instant, fortified, with raisins and spice, prepared with water	240	1.0 cup	211	4.75	42.98
Cereals, QUAKER, Instant Oatmeal Organic, Regular	41	1.0 packet	150	6.56	27.47
Cereals, QUAKER, QUAKER MultiGrain Oatmeal, dry	40	0.5 cup (1 NLEA serving)	134	5.06	29.05
Cereals, ready-to-eat, MALT-O-MEAL, Blueberry Mini SPOONERS	55	1.0 cup (1 NLEA serving)	192	4.85	43.67
Cereals, WHEATENA, cooked with water	243	1.0 cup	136	4.86	28.67

Fats and Oils

Description	Weight (g)	Measure	Energy (kcal)	Protein (g)	Carbohydrate, by difference (g)
Fat, beef tallow	12.8	1.0 tbsp	115	0	--
Margarine-like, margarine-butter blend, soybean oil and butter	14.1	1.0 tbsp	103	0.04	0.11
Oil, canola	14	1.0 tbsp	124	0	--
Oil, cocoa butter	13.6	1.0 tablespoon	120	0	--
Oil, mustard	14	1.0 tbsp	124	0	--
Oil, olive, salad or cooking	13.5	1.0 tablespoon	119	0	--
Oil, safflower, salad or cooking, linoleic, (over 70%)	13.6	1.0 tbsp	120	0	--
Oil, sesame, salad or cooking	13.6	1.0 tablespoon	120	0	--
Oil, soybean, salad or cooking, (partially hydrogenated) and cottonseed	13.6	1.0 tablespoon	120	0	--
Oil, sunflower, high oleic (70% and over)	14	1.0 tbsp	124	0	--
Salad dressing, french, home recipe	14	1.0 tablespoon	88	0.01	0.48
Salad dressing, KRAFT Mayo Fat Free Mayonnaise Dressing	16	1.0 tbsp	10	0.03	2.53
Salad dressing, mayonnaise type, regular, with salt	14.7	1.0 tbsp	37	0.1	2.17
Salad dressing, mayonnaise, imitation, milk cream	15	1.0 tablespoon	15	0.32	1.67
Salad dressing, mayonnaise, imitation, soybean	15	1.0 tbsp	35	0.04	2.4
Salad dressing, mayonnaise, regular	13.8	1.0 tbsp	94	0.13	0.08
Salad dressing, mayonnaise, soybean and safflower oil, with salt	13.8	1.0 tablespoon	99	0.15	0.37
Salad dressing, russian dressing, low calorie	16	1.0 tablespoon	23	0.08	4.42
Salad dressing, sesame seed dressing, regular	15	1.0 tablespoon	66	0.47	1.29
Salad dressing, thousand island dressing, reduced fat	15	1.0 tablespoon	29	0.12	3.61
Shortening bread, soybean (hydrogenated) and cottonseed	12.8	1.0 tablespoon	113	0	--

Nuts and Seeds

Description	Weight (g)	Measure	Energy (kcal)	Protein (g)	Carbohydrate, by difference (g)
Nuts, almond butter, plain, with salt added	16	1.0 tbsp	98	3.35	3.01
Nuts, almonds, dry roasted, without salt added	138	1.0 cup whole kernels	825	28.92	28.99
Nuts, butternuts, dried	120	1.0 cup	734	29.88	14.46
Nuts, chestnuts, chinese, boiled and steamed	28.4	1.0 oz	43	0.82	9.54
Nuts, chestnuts, european, raw, unpeeled	145	1.0 cup	309	3.51	66.03
Nuts, coconut cream, canned, sweetened	19	1.0 tbsp	68	0.22	10.11
Nuts, coconut cream, raw (liquid expressed from grated meat)	15	1.0 tbsp	50	0.54	1
Nuts, coconut meat, dried (desiccated), not sweetened	28.4	1.0 oz	187	1.95	6.7
Nuts, coconut meat, dried (desiccated), sweetened, flaked, packaged	85	1.0 cup	388	2.66	44.07
Nuts, coconut meat, dried (desiccated), toasted	28.4	1.0 oz	168	1.5	12.59
Nuts, hazelnuts or filberts	115	1.0 cup, chopped	722	17.19	19.2
Nuts, mixed nuts, oil roasted, with peanuts, lightly salted	28.4	1.0 oz	172	5.68	5.97
Seeds, lotus seeds, dried	32	1.0 cup	106	4.93	20.63
Seeds, pumpkin and squash seed kernels, roasted, with salt added	118	1.0 cup	677	35.21	17.36
Seeds, safflower seed meal, partially defatted	28.4	1.0 oz	97	10.1	13.81
Seeds, sesame flour, low-fat	28.4	1.0 oz	94	14.21	10.07
Seeds, sunflower seed kernels, oil roasted, without salt	135	1.0 cup	799	27.08	30.9
Seeds, sunflower seed kernels, toasted, without salt	134	1.0 cup	829	23.06	27.59

Legumes

Description	Weight (g)	Measure	Energy (kcal)	Protein (g)	Carbohydrate, by difference (g)
Beans, adzuki, mature seeds, raw	197	1.0 cup	648	39.14	123.91
Beans, baked, canned, with pork	253	1.0 cup	268	13.13	50.57
Beans, black turtle, mature seeds, canned	240	1.0 cup	218	14.47	39.72
Beans, black turtle, mature seeds, cooked, boiled, without salt	185	1.0 cup	240	15.13	45.05
Beans, black, mature seeds, raw	194	1.0 cup	662	41.9	120.98
Beans, pink, mature seeds, raw	210	1.0 cup	720	44.02	134.8
LOMA LINDA Linketts, canned, unprepared	35	1.0 link	73	7.46	1.54
LOMA LINDA Swiss Stake with Gravy, canned, unprepared	92	1.0 piece	127	9.38	9.57
MORI-NU, Tofu, silken, firm	84	1.0 slice	52	5.8	2.02
MORNINGSTAR FARMS Buffalo Chik Patties, frozen, unprepared	71	1.0 patty	181	8.59	17.89
Peanuts, all types, dry-roasted, without salt	146	1.0 cup	857	35.55	31.04
Peanuts, valencia, oil-roasted, without salt	144	1.0 cup	848	38.94	23.47
Tofu, raw, firm, prepared with calcium sulfate	126	0.5 cup	181	21.76	3.5

Sausage and Luncheon Meats

Description	Weight (g)	Measure	Energy (kcal)	Protein(g)	Carbohydrate, by difference(g)
Bacon and beef sticks	28	1.0 oz	145	8.15	0.22
Barbecue loaf, pork, beef	28.4	1.0 oz	49	4.49	1.81
Beerwurst, beer salami, pork and beef	56	2.0 oz	155	7.84	2.11
Beerwurst, pork and beef	56	1.0 serving 2 oz	155	7.84	2.39
Bologna, chicken, turkey, pork	28	1.0 serving	83	2.77	1.58
Bologna, meat and poultry	33	1.0 slice	93	3.41	2.08
Bologna, pork and turkey, lite	56	1.0 serving 2 oz	118	7.31	1.93
Bologna, pork, turkey and beef	28.4	1.0 oz	95	3.28	1.89
Bratwurst, pork, beef and turkey, lite, smoked	66	1.0 serving 2.33 oz	123	9.54	1.07
Braunschweiger (a liver sausage), pork	28.4	1.0 oz	93	4.11	0.88
Chicken breast, oven-roasted, fat-free, sliced	42	1.0 serving 2 slices	33	7.05	0.91
Frankfurter, meat	52	1.0 serving (1 hot dog)	151	5.34	2.17
Frankfurter, pork	76	1.0 link	204	9.74	0.21
Ham, honey, smoked, cooked	55	1.94 oz (1 serving)	67	9.86	4
HORMEL Pillow Pak Sliced Turkey Pepperoni	30	1.0 serving	73	9.3	1.13
Kielbasa, Polish, turkey and beef, smoked	56	1.0 serving 2 oz	127	7.34	2.18
Liverwurst spread	55	0.25 cup	168	6.81	3.24
Luncheon meat, pork, ham, and chicken, minced, canned, reduced sodium, added ascorbic acid, includes SPAM, 25% less sodium	56	2.0 oz 1 NLEA serving	164	7	1.9
Pastrami, beef, 98% fat-free	57	1.0 serving 6 slices	54	11.17	0.88
Pork and turkey sausage, pre-cooked	57	1.0 serving	195	6.87	2.07
Pork sausage, link/patty, fully cooked, unheated	23	1.0 link	90	3.1	0.16
Pork sausage, link/patty, reduced fat, unprepared	85	3.0 oz	184	14.24	0.17
Salami, Italian, pork	28	1.0 oz	119	6.08	0.34
Salami, pork, beef, less sodium	100	3.527 oz	396	15.01	15.38
Sausage, chicken, beef, pork, skinless, smoked	84	1.0 link	181	11.42	6.8
Sausage, Italian, sweet, links	84	1.0 link 3 oz	125	13.55	1.76
Sausage, pork and beef, with cheddar cheese, smoked	77	12.0 oz serving 2.7 oz	228	9.93	1.64
Sausage, turkey, hot, smoked	56	2.0 oz	88	8.43	2.6
Turkey sausage, fresh, raw	57	1.0 serving	88	10.71	0.27
Turkey, breast, smoked, lemon pepper flavor, 97% fat-free	28	1.0 slice	27	5.85	0.37
Turkey, white, rotisserie, deli cut	48	1.69 oz (1 serving)	54	6.48	3.7
USDA Commodity, pork sausage, bulk/links/patties, frozen, raw	28	1.0 link	65	4.19	0

113

Poultry

Description	Weight (g)	Measure	Energy (kcal)	Protein (g)	Carbohydrate, by difference(g)
Chicken, broiler, rotisserie, BBQ, back meat only	85	3.0 oz	180	18.57	0.26
Chicken, broilers or fryers, back, meat and skin, raw	59	1.0 unit (yield from 1 lb ready-to-cook chicken)	188	8.29	0
Chicken, broilers or fryers, back, meat only, raw	31	1.0 unit (yield from 1 lb ready-to-cook chicken)	42	6.06	0
Chicken, broilers or fryers, dark meat, meat and skin, cooked, stewed	110	1.0 unit (yield from 1 lb ready-to-cook chicken)	256	25.85	0
Chicken, broilers or fryers, dark meat, meat only, cooked, fried	140	1.0 cup	335	40.59	3.63
Chicken, broilers or fryers, drumstick, meat and skin, cooked, stewed	140	1.0 cup, chopped or diced	286	35.45	0
Chicken, broilers or fryers, drumstick, meat only, cooked, fried	25	1.0 unit (yield from 1 lb ready-to-cook chicken)	49	7.16	0
Chicken, broilers or fryers, giblets, raw	23	1.0 unit (yield from 1 lb ready-to-cook chicken)	29	4.11	0.41
Chicken, broilers or fryers, leg, meat and skin, cooked, roasted	85	3.0 oz	156	20.43	0
Chicken, broilers or fryers, leg, meat only, cooked, fried	56	1.0 unit (yield from 1 lb ready-to-cook chicken)	116	15.89	0.36
Chicken, broilers or fryers, light meat, meat only, raw	88	1.0 unit (yield from 1 lb ready-to-cook chicken)	100	20.42	0
Chicken, broilers or fryers, meat and skin and giblets and neck, cooked, fried, batter	85	3.0 oz	247	19.41	7.68
Chicken, broilers or fryers, meat and skin, cooked, fried, flour	85	3.0 oz	229	24.28	2.68
Chicken, broilers or fryers, separable fat, raw	12.8	1.0 tbsp	81	0.48	0
Chicken, broilers or fryers, wing, meat only, raw	17	1.0 wing, bone and skin removed (yield from 1 lb ready-to-cook chicken)	21	3.73	0
Chicken, dark meat, thigh, meat only, with added solution, raw	85	3.0 oz	94	16.24	0
Chicken, gizzard, all classes, cooked, simmered	145	1.0 cup chopped or dice	223	44.07	0
Chicken, skin (drumsticks and thighs), raw	28.4	1.0 oz	125	2.72	0.22
Chicken, stewing, meat and skin, and giblets and neck, cooked, stewed	85	3.0 oz	182	21.15	0
Ground turkey, 93% lean, 7% fat, pan-broiled crumbles	85	3.0 oz	181	23.04	0

114

Description	Weight (g)	Measure	Energy (kcal)	Protein (g)	Carbohydrate, by difference(g)
Ground turkey, fat free, patties, broiled	85	1.0 patty	117	24.64	0
Guinea hen, meat only, raw	85	3.0 oz	94	17.54	0
Squab, (pigeon), meat and skin, raw	85	3.0 oz	250	15.7	0
Turkey from whole, light meat, meat only, with added solution, cooked, roasted	85	3.0 oz	108	22.92	0
Turkey, all classes, back, meat and skin, cooked, roasted	140	1.0 cup, chopped or diced	342	37.23	0.22
Turkey, all classes, leg, meat and skin, cooked, roasted	71	1.0 unit (yield from 1 lb ready-to-cook turkey)	148	19.79	0
Turkey, breast, from whole bird, meat only, roasted	85	3.0 oz	125	25.61	0
Turkey, dark meat from whole, meat and skin, cooked, roasted	85	1.0 serving	175	23.18	0.06
Turkey, drumstick, from whole bird, meat only, raw	85	3.0 oz	93	20.11	0.12
Turkey, retail parts, thigh, meat and skin, cooked, roasted	85	3.0 oz	156	20.36	0.35

Pork					
Description	Weight (g)	Measure	Energy (kcal)	Protein (g)	Carbohydrate, by difference(g)
Pork, cured, ham and water product, slice, boneless, separable lean and fat, heated, pan-broil	136	1.0 slice	169	20.51	6.38
Pork, cured, ham with natural juices, spiral slice, boneless, separable lean and fat, heated, roasted	145	1.0 slice	202	32.16	1.54
Pork, cured, ham, rump, bone-in, separable lean and fat, unheated	85	3.0 oz	150	18.93	0.44
Pork, cured, ham, rump, bone-in, separable lean only, unheated	28.4	1.0 oz	35	6.93	0.09
Pork, cured, ham, shank, bone-in, separable lean and fat, unheated	28.4	1.0 oz	50	6.13	0.12
Pork, cured, ham, shank, bone-in, separable lean only, unheated	28.4	1.0 oz	35	6.74	0.05
Pork, fresh, enhanced, loin, tenderloin, separable lean only, raw	85	3.0 oz	90	17.33	0
Pork, fresh, leg (ham), whole, separable lean and fat, raw	28.4	1.0 oz	69	4.94	0
Pork, fresh, leg (ham), whole, separable lean only, cooked, roasted	135	1.0 cup, diced	285	39.7	0
Pork, fresh, loin, blade (chops or roasts), boneless, separable lean and fat only, raw	85	3.0 oz	133	17.46	0.65
Pork, fresh, loin, blade (chops or roasts), boneless, separable lean only, raw	85	3.0 oz	105	18.15	0.7
Pork, fresh, loin, blade (chops), boneless, separable lean only, boneless, cooked, broiled	85	3.0 oz	144	22.22	0.76
Pork, fresh, loin, blade (roasts), boneless, separable lean and fat, cooked, roasted	85	3.0 oz	169	22.51	0

Description	Weight (g)	Measure	Energy (kcal)	Protein (g)	Carbohydrate, by difference(g)
Pork, fresh, loin, center rib (roasts), bone-in, separable lean only, cooked, roasted	85	3.0 oz	175	24.5	0
Pork, fresh, loin, country-style ribs, separable lean and fat, bone-in, cooked, broiled	122	1.0 rack	317	31.21	0
Pork, fresh, loin, country-style ribs, separable lean only, bone-in, cooked, broiled	122	1.0 rack	264	33.95	0
Pork, fresh, loin, sirloin (roasts), bone-in, separable lean and fat, cooked, roasted	85	3.0 oz	196	22.64	0
Pork, fresh, loin, tenderloin, separable lean and fat, with added solution, raw	85	3.0 oz	97	17.14	0
Pork, fresh, loin, top loin (roasts), boneless, separable lean only, cooked, roasted	85	3.0 oz	147	23.15	0
Pork, fresh, loin, whole, separable lean and fat, cooked, broiled	85	3.0 oz	206	23.22	0
Pork, fresh, shoulder, (Boston butt), blade (steaks), separable lean and fat, with added solution, cooked, braised	85	3.0 oz	224	21.96	0.03
Pork, fresh, shoulder, (Boston butt), blade (steaks), separable lean and fat,with added solution, raw	85	3.0 oz	144	14.61	0.14
Pork, fresh, shoulder, blade, boston (roasts), separable lean and fat, cooked, roasted	85	3.0 oz	229	19.64	0
Pork, fresh, shoulder, blade, boston (steaks), separable lean only, cooked, broiled	85	3.0 oz	193	22.73	0
Pork, fresh, shoulder, whole, separable lean and fat, cooked, roasted	135	1.0 cup, diced	394	31.43	0
Pork, fresh, variety meats and by-products, brain, cooked, braised	85	3.0 oz	117	10.32	0
Pork, fresh, variety meats and by-products, feet, raw	28.4	1.0 oz	60	6.57	0
Pork, fresh, variety meats and by-products, pancreas, raw	28.4	1.0 oz	56	5.26	0
Pork, ground, 96% lean / 4% fat, cooked, crumbles	85	3.0 oz grilled patties	159	25.97	0
Pork, ground, 96% lean / 4% fat, raw	113	4.0 oz	137	23.84	0.24
Pork, Leg sirloin tip roast, boneless, separable lean and fat, raw	85	3.0 oz	96	19.45	0

Beef					
Description	Weight (g)	Measure	Energy (kcal)	Protein (g)	Carbohydrate, by difference(g)
Beef, Australian, imported, grass-fed, loin, tenderloin steak/roast, boneless, separable lean and fat, raw	114	4.0 oz	172	23.4	0.01
Beef, Australian, imported, grass-fed, seam fat, raw	28.4	1.0 oz	159	2.72	0.3
Beef, brisket, flat half, boneless, separable lean and fat, trimmed to 0" fat, choice, raw	85	3.0 oz	144	17.13	0
Beef, brisket, flat half, separable lean and fat, trimmed to 0" fat, select, cooked, braised	85	3.0 oz	174	28.55	0
Beef, chuck eye roast, boneless, America's Beef Roast, separable lean and fat, trimmed to 0" fat, all grades, raw	85	3.0 oz	153	16.3	0

Food	Weight (g)	Serving	Calories	Protein	
Beef, chuck, short ribs, boneless, separable lean only, trimmed to 0" fat, choice, cooked, braised	85	3.0 oz	212	24.51	0
Beef, chuck, top blade, separable lean only, trimmed to 0" fat, select, cooked, broiled	85	3.0 oz	156	22.24	0
Beef, flank, steak, separable lean and fat, trimmed to 0" fat, all grades, raw	85	3.0 oz	132	18.04	0
Beef, ground, 90% lean meat / 10% fat, patty, cooked, broiled	85	3.0 oz	184	22.19	0
Beef, loin, bottom sirloin butt, tri-tip roast, separable lean only, trimmed to 0" fat, all grades, cooked, roasted	85	1.0 serving	155	22.74	0
Beef, loin, top loin, separable lean and fat, trimmed to 1/8" fat, select, raw	85	3.0 oz	190	17.5	0
Beef, loin, top sirloin petite roast, boneless, separable lean only, trimmed to 0" fat, select, cooked, roasted	85	3.0 oz	140	24.95	0
Beef, rib, small end (ribs 10-12), separable lean and fat, trimmed to 1/8" fat, choice, cooked, roasted	85	3.0 oz	305	18.94	0
Beef, ribeye petite roast/filet, boneless, separable lean only, trimmed to 0" fat, select, raw	85	3.0 oz	106	19.46	0
Beef, ribeye cap steak, boneless, separable lean only, trimmed to 0" fat, choice, raw	85	3.0 oz	159	16.54	1.49
Beef, round, top round steak, boneless, separable lean and fat, trimmed to 0" fat, all grades, cooked, grilled	85	3.0 oz	142	25.47	0
Beef, round, top round steak, boneless, separable lean and fat, trimmed to 0" fat, choice, cooked, grilled	85	3.0 oz	144	25.6	0
Beef, round, top round, separable lean and fat, trimmed to 1/8" fat, select, cooked, braised	85	3.0 oz	191	29.41	0
Beef, round, top round, steak, separable lean and fat, trimmed to 1/8" fat, choice, cooked, broiled	85	3.0 oz	190	26.09	0
Beef, round, top round, steak, separable lean and fat, trimmed to 1/8" fat, prime, cooked, broiled	85	3.0 oz	191	26.58	0
Beef, shank crosscuts, separable lean only, trimmed to 1/4" fat, choice, cooked, simmered	85	3.0 oz	171	28.63	0
Beef, short loin, porterhouse steak, separable lean and fat, trimmed to 1/8" fat, choice, raw	85	3.0 oz	185	17.31	0
Beef, short loin, porterhouse steak, separable lean only, trimmed to 0" fat, choice, cooked, broiled	85	3.0 oz	190	21.68	0
Beef, tenderloin, steak, separable lean and fat, trimmed to 1/8" fat, all grades, cooked, broiled	85	3.0 oz	227	22.49	0
Beef, tenderloin, steak, separable lean and fat, trimmed to 1/8" fat, select, raw	149	1.0 steak (yield from 1 raw steak weighing149g)	371	20.86	0
Beef, top loin petite roast/filet, boneless, separable lean and fat, trimmed to 1/8" fat, all grades, raw	85	3.0 oz	159	17.94	0.26
Beef, top sirloin, steak, separable lean and fat, trimmed to 1/8" fat, choice, cooked, broiled	85	3.0 oz	218	22.78	0
Beef, top sirloin, steak, separable lean only, trimmed to 0" fat, choice, cooked, broiled	85	3.0 oz	160	25.75	0

Vegetables and Vegetable Products

Description	Weight (g)	Measure	Energy (kcal)	Protein (g)	Carbohydrate, by difference(g)
Amaranth leaves, cooked, boiled, drained, without salt	132	1.0 cup	28	2.79	5.43
Arrowhead, cooked, boiled, drained, without salt	12	1.0 medium	9	0.54	1.94
Arugula, raw	2	1.0 leaf	0	0.05	0.07
Asparagus, canned, drained solids	242	1.0 cup	46	5.18	5.95
Asparagus, canned, regular pack, solids and liquids	122	0.5 cup	18	2.2	3.03
Asparagus, cooked, boiled, drained	90	0.5 cup	20	2.16	3.7
Asparagus, frozen, cooked, boiled, drained, without salt	180	1.0 cup	32	5.31	3.46
Balsam-pear (bitter gourd), pods, raw	93	1.0 cup (1/2" pieces)	16	0.93	3.44
Bamboo shoots, raw	151	1.0 cup (1/2" slices)	41	3.93	7.85
Beans, kidney, mature seeds, sprouted, raw	184	1.0 cup	53	7.73	7.54
Beans, pinto, immature seeds, frozen, unprepared	94	0.333 package (10 oz)	160	9.21	30.55
Beans, snap, green, frozen, cooked, boiled, drained without salt	135	1.0 cup	38	2.01	8.71
Beet greens, raw	38	1.0 cup	8	0.84	1.65
Beets, canned, regular pack, solids and liquids	246	1.0 cup	74	1.8	17.56
Beets, raw	136	1.0 cup	58	2.19	13
Broccoli raab, raw	40	1.0 cup chopped	9	1.27	1.14
Broccoli, frozen, chopped, cooked, boiled, drained, without salt	184	1.0 cup	52	5.7	9.84
Broccoli, frozen, chopped, unprepared	156	1.0 cup	41	4.38	7.46
Brussels sprouts, raw	88	1.0 cup	38	2.97	7.88
Burdock root, cooked, boiled, drained, without salt	125	1.0 cup (1" pieces)	110	2.61	26.44
Cabbage, chinese (pak-choi), cooked, boiled, drained, with salt	170	1.0 cup, shredded	20	2.65	3.03
Cabbage, chinese (pak-choi), cooked, boiled, drained, without salt	170	1.0 cup, shredded	20	2.65	3.03
Cabbage, chinese (pe-tsai), raw	76	1.0 cup, shredded	12	0.91	2.45
Cardoon, raw	178	1.0 cup, shredded	30	1.25	7.24
Carrots, canned, no salt added, solids and liquids	123	0.5 cup slices	28	0.73	6.59
Carrots, canned, regular pack, drained solids	146	1.0 cup, sliced	36	0.93	8.09
Carrots, frozen, unprepared	64	0.5 cup slices	23	0.5	5.06
Carrots, raw	128	1.0 cup chopped	52	1.19	12.26
Cauliflower, green, raw	64	1.0 cup	20	1.89	3.9
Celery, cooked, boiled, drained, without salt	150	1.0 cup, diced	27	1.25	6
Chicory roots, raw	60	1.0 root	43	0.84	10.51
Chicory, witloof, raw	53	1.0 head	9	0.48	2.12

Collards, frozen, chopped, unprepared	95	0.33 package (10 oz)	31	2.56	6.14
Corn, sweet, yellow, canned, brine pack, regular pack, solids and liquids	256	1.0 cup	156	4.99	35.48
Corn, sweet, yellow, canned, drained solids, rinsed with tap water	150	1.0 cup drained, rinsed	111	3.27	19.53
Corn, sweet, yellow, canned, vacuum pack, regular pack	210	1.0 cup	166	5.06	40.82
Corn, sweet, yellow, frozen, kernels cut off cob, boiled, drained, without salt	165	1.0 cup	134	4.21	31.84
Corn, sweet, yellow, frozen, kernels cut off cob, unprepared	136	1.0 cup	120	4.11	28.17
Cowpeas (blackeyes), immature seeds, cooked, boiled, drained, without salt	165	1.0 cup	160	5.23	33.53
Cowpeas (blackeyes), immature seeds, frozen, cooked, boiled, drained, without salt	170	1.0 cup	224	14.43	40.39
Cowpeas (blackeyes), immature seeds, raw	145	1.0 cup	130	4.28	27.3
Cowpeas, leafy tips, raw	36	1.0 cup, chopped	10	1.48	1.74
Cress, garden, raw	50	1.0 cup	16	1.3	2.75
Drumstick pods, raw	100	1.0 cup slices	37	2.1	8.53
Edamame, frozen, unprepared	110	1.0 cup	129	13.24	0.98
Endive, raw	25	0.5 cup, chopped	4	0.31	0.84
Garlic, raw	136	1.0 cup	203	8.65	44.96
Ginger root, raw	2	1.0 tsp	2	0.04	0.36
Gourd, white-flowered (calabash), raw	58	0.5 cup (1" pieces)	8	0.36	1.97
Hyacinth-beans, immature seeds, cooked, boiled, drained, without salt	87	1.0 cup	44	2.57	8
Jute, potherb, cooked, boiled, drained, without salt	87	1.0 cup	32	3.2	6.34
Kale, frozen, unprepared	94	0.333 package (10 oz)	26	2.5	4.61
Kale, raw	16	1.0 cup 1" pieces, loosely packed	8	0.68	1.4
Kanpyo, (dried gourd strips)	6.3	1.0 strip	16	0.54	4.1
Leeks, (bulb and lower leaf-portion), cooked, boiled, drained, without salt	124	1.0 leek	38	1	9.45
Lima beans, immature seeds, cooked, boiled, drained, without salt	170	1.0 cup	209	11.58	40.19
Lima beans, immature seeds, frozen, baby, cooked, boiled, drained, without salt	180	1.0 cup	189	11.97	35.01
Lima beans, immature seeds, frozen, baby, unprepared	164	1.0 cup	216	12.45	41.23
Lima beans, immature seeds, frozen, fordhook, unprepared	160	1.0 cup	170	10.24	31.73
Mountain yam, hawaii, cooked, steamed, without salt	145	1.0 cup, cubes	119	2.51	29
Mountain yam, hawaii, raw	68	0.5 cup, cubes	46	0.91	11.08
Mung beans, mature seeds, sprouted, cooked, boiled, drained, without salt	124	1.0 cup	26	2.52	5.2

Mushrooms, Chanterelle, raw	54	1.0 cup	21	0.8	3.7
Mushrooms, portabella, grilled	121	1.0 cup sliced	35	3.97	5.37
Okra, frozen, cooked, boiled, drained, without salt	92	0.5 cup slices	27	1.5	5.9
Okra, frozen, unprepared	95	0.33 package (10 oz)	28	1.61	6.3
Onions, dehydrated flakes	5	1.0 tbsp	17	0.45	4.16
Onions, frozen, chopped, cooked, boiled, drained, without salt	15	1.0 tbsp chopped	4	0.12	0.99
Onions, frozen, chopped, unprepared	95	0.33 package (10 oz)	28	0.75	6.48
Onions, frozen, whole, cooked, boiled, drained, without salt	210	1.0 cup	59	1.49	14.07
Onions, frozen, whole, unprepared	95	0.33 package (10 oz)	33	0.85	8.03
Onions, raw	160	1.0 cup, chopped	64	1.76	14.94
Onions, sweet, raw	148	1.0 NLEA serving	47	1.18	11.17
Peas and carrots, frozen, cooked, boiled, drained, without salt	278	1.0 package (10 oz) yields	133	8.59	28.13
Peas, edible-podded, frozen, unprepared	144	1.0 cup	60	4.03	10.37
Peas, edible-podded, raw	98	1.0 cup, chopped	41	2.74	7.4
Peas, green, raw	145	1.0 cup	117	7.86	20.95
Peas, mature seeds, sprouted, raw	120	1.0 cup	149	10.56	32.53
Peppers, pasilla, dried	7	1.0 pepper	24	0.86	3.58
Peppers, sweet, green, freeze-dried	0.4	1.0 tbsp	1	0.07	0.27
Pokeberry shoots, (poke), cooked, boiled, drained, without salt	165	1.0 cup	33	3.79	5.12
Potatoes, baked, skin, without salt	58	1.0 skin	115	2.49	26.71
Potatoes, boiled, cooked without skin, flesh, with salt	78	0.5 cup	67	1.33	15.61
Potatoes, boiled, cooked without skin, flesh, without salt	78	0.5 cup	67	1.33	15.61
Potatoes, flesh and skin, raw	75	0.5 cup, diced	58	1.54	13.12
Potatoes, french fried, cottage-cut, salt not added in processing, frozen, as purchased	65	10.0 strips	99	1.57	15.59
Potatoes, mashed, dehydrated, flakes without milk, dry form	60	1.0 cup	212	5	48.7
Potatoes, mashed, dehydrated, prepared from flakes without milk, whole milk and butter added	210	1.0 cup	204	3.72	22.83
Potatoes, mashed, dehydrated, prepared from granules with milk, water and margarine added	210	1.0 cup	244	4.47	33.87
Potatoes, mashed, dehydrated, prepared from granules without milk, whole milk and butter added	210	1.0 cup	227	4.3	30.16
Potatoes, roasted, salt added in processing, frozen, unprepared	85	3.0 oz	110	1.89	22.23
Potatoes, Russet, flesh and skin, baked	299	1.0 potato large (3" to 4-1/4" dia.	290	7.86	64.11

Potatoes, scalloped, home-prepared with butter	245	1.0 cup	216	7.03	26.41
Purslane, cooked, boiled, drained, without salt	115	1.0 cup	21	1.71	4.08
Purslane, raw	43	1.0 cup	9	0.87	1.46
Radishes, raw	116	1.0 cup slices	19	0.79	3.94
Sesbania flower, raw	3	1.0 flower	1	0.04	0.2
Soybeans, green, cooked, boiled, drained, without salt	180	1.0 cup	254	22.23	19.89
Soybeans, green, raw	256	1.0 cup	376	33.15	28.29
Soybeans, mature seeds, sprouted, cooked, steamed	94	1.0 cup	76	7.96	6.14
Spinach, canned, regular pack, solids and liquids	234	1.0 cup	44	4.94	6.83
Spinach, raw	30	1.0 cup	7	0.86	1.09
Squash, summer, crookneck and straightneck, frozen, cooked, boiled, drained, without salt	192	1.0 cup slices	48	2.46	10.64
Squash, summer, zucchini, includes skin, cooked, boiled, drained, without salt	180	1.0 cup, sliced	27	2.05	4.84
Squash, summer, zucchini, italian style, canned	227	1.0 cup	66	2.34	15.55
Squash, winter, acorn, cooked, boiled, mashed, with salt	245	1.0 cup, mashed	83	1.64	21.54
Squash, winter, acorn, cooked, boiled, mashed, without salt	245	1.0 cup, mashed	83	1.64	21.54
Squash, winter, butternut, cooked, baked, without salt	205	1.0 cup, cubes	82	1.84	21.5
Squash, winter, butternut, frozen, cooked, boiled, without salt	240	1.0 cup, mashed	94	2.95	24.12
Squash, winter, hubbard, baked, with salt	205	1.0 cup, cubes	102	5.08	22.16
Squash, winter, hubbard, cooked, boiled, mashed, with salt	236	1.0 cup, mashed	71	3.49	15.25
Squash, winter, hubbard, cooked, boiled, mashed, without salt	236	1.0 cup, mashed	71	3.49	15.25
Swamp cabbage (skunk cabbage), cooked, boiled, drained, with salt	98	1.0 cup, chopped	20	2.04	3.63
Sweet potato, canned, syrup pack, drained solids	196	1.0 cup	212	2.51	49.71
Sweet potato, cooked, baked in skin, flesh, with salt	114	1.0 medium (2" dia, 5" long, raw)	105	2.29	23.61
Taro, tahitian, cooked, without salt	137	1.0 cup slices	60	5.7	9.38
Tomato juice, canned, with salt added	243	1.0 cup	41	2.07	8.58
Tomato juice, canned, without salt added	243	1.0 cup	41	2.07	0.50
Tomato products, canned, puree, with salt added	250	1.0 cup	95	4.12	22.45
Tomato products, canned, puree, without salt added	250	1.0 cup	95	4.12	22.45
Tomato products, canned, sauce, with onions	245	1.0 cup	103	3.82	24.35
Tomato products, canned, sauce, with onions, green peppers, and celery	250	1.0 cup	102	2.35	21.93

Description	Weight (g)	Measure	Energy (kcal)	Protein (g)	Carbohydrate, by difference (g)
Tomato products, canned, sauce, with tomato tidbits	244	1.0 cup	78	3.22	17.3
Tomatoes, red, ripe, canned, packed in tomato juice	240	1.0 cup	38	1.9	8.33
Tomatoes, red, ripe, canned, stewed	255	1.0 cup	66	2.32	15.78
Tree fern, cooked, without salt	71	0.5 cup, chopped	28	0.21	7.8
Turnip greens and turnips, frozen, cooked, boiled, drained, with salt	163	1.0 cup	55	4.87	7.73
Turnip greens, cooked, boiled, drained, without salt	144	1.0 cup, chopped	29	1.64	6.28
Turnip greens, frozen, cooked, boiled, drained, with salt	82	0.5 cup	24	2.75	4.08
Turnip greens, frozen, cooked, boiled, drained, without salt	164	1.0 cup	48	5.49	8.17
Turnip greens, frozen, unprepared	82	0.5 cup, chopped or diced	18	2.03	3.01
Turnips, frozen, cooked, boiled, drained, without salt	156	1.0 cup	36	2.39	6.79
Vegetable juice cocktail, canned	253	1.0 cup	56	2.35	9.79
Yardlong bean, cooked, boiled, drained, without salt	104	1.0 cup slices	49	2.63	9.55

Fruits and Fruit Juices

Description	Weight (g)	Measure	Energy (kcal)	Protein (g)	Carbohydrate, by difference (g)
Apples, frozen, unsweetened, unheated	173	1.0 cup slices	83	0.48	21.3
Apples, raw, without skin	110	1.0 cup slices	53	0.3	14.04
Applesauce, canned, sweetened, without salt (includes USDA commodity)	246	1.0 cup	167	0.39	43.03
Apricots, canned, heavy syrup pack, with skin, solids and liquids	258	1.0 cup, halves	214	1.37	55.39
Apricots, canned, heavy syrup, drained	219	1.0 cup, halves	182	1.4	46.67
Apricots, dehydrated (low-moisture), sulfured, uncooked	119	1.0 cup	381	5.83	98.64
Apricots, dried, sulfured, stewed, without added sugar	250	1.0 cup, halves	212	3	55.38
Blackberries, frozen, unsweetened	151	1.0 cup, unthawed	97	1.78	23.66
Blackberry juice, canned	250	1.0 cup	95	0.75	19.5
Blueberries, frozen, sweetened	230	1.0 cup, thawed	196	0.92	50.48
Blueberries, wild, canned, heavy syrup, drained	319	1.0 cup	341	1.79	90.34
Boysenberries, canned, heavy syrup	256	1.0 cup	225	2.53	57.11
Boysenberries, frozen, unsweetened	132	1.0 cup, unthawed	66	1.45	16.09
Breadfruit, raw	220	1.0 cup	227	2.35	59.66
Carambola, (starfruit), raw	132	1.0 cup, cubes	41	1.37	8.88
Carissa, (natal-plum), raw	150	1.0 cup slices	93	0.75	20.45
Cherries, sour, red, canned, light syrup pack, solids and liquids	252	1.0 cup	189	1.86	48.64
Cherries, sour, red, frozen, unsweetened	155	1.0 cup, unthawed	71	1.43	17.08
Cherries, sweet, canned, water pack, solids and liquids	248	1.0 cup, pitted	114	1.91	29.16

Cherries, sweet, raw	138	1.0 cup, with pits, yields	87	1.46	22.09
Cranberry sauce, canned, sweetened	277	1.0 cup	440	2.49	111.91
Currants, european black, raw	112	1.0 cup	71	1.57	17.23
Currants, red and white, raw	112	1.0 cup	63	1.57	15.46
Currants, zante, dried	144	1.0 cup	408	5.88	106.68
Figs, canned, water pack, solids and liquids	248	1.0 cup	131	0.99	34.7
Figs, raw	64	1.0 large (2-1/2" dia)	47	0.48	12.28
Fruit cocktail, (peach and pineapple and pear and grape and cherry), canned, extra light syrup, solids and liquids	123	0.5 cup	55	0.49	14.3
Fruit cocktail, (peach and pineapple and pear and grape and cherry), canned, heavy syrup, solids and liquids	248	1.0 cup	181	0.97	46.9
Fruit salad, (peach and pear and apricot and pineapple and cherry), canned, heavy syrup, solids and liquids	255	1.0 cup	186	0.87	48.73
Fruit salad, (peach and pear and apricot and pineapple and cherry), canned, water pack, solids and liquids	245	1.0 cup	74	0.86	19.28
Gooseberries, raw	150	1.0 cup	66	1.32	15.27
Grapefruit juice, white, canned, sweetened	250	1.0 cup	115	1.45	27.82
Grapefruit juice, white, frozen concentrate, unsweetened, undiluted	207	1.0 can (6 fl oz)	302	4.08	71.54
Grapefruit, raw, pink and red, all areas	230	1.0 cup sections, with juice	97	1.77	24.52
Grapefruit, raw, white, Florida	230	1.0 cup sections, with juice	74	1.45	18.84
Grapefruit, sections, canned, juice pack, solids and liquids	249	1.0 cup	92	1.74	22.93
Grapefruit, sections, canned, water pack, solids and liquids	244	1.0 cup	88	1.42	22.33
Grapes, american type (slip skin), raw	92	1.0 cup	62	0.58	15.78
Grapes, canned, thompson seedless, water pack, solids and liquids	245	1.0 cup	98	1.23	25.23
Grapes, muscadine, raw	6	1.0 grape	3	0.05	0.84
Groundcherries, (cape-gooseberries or poha), raw	140	1.0 cup	74	2.66	15.68
Kiwifruit, green, raw	180	1.0 cup, sliced	110	2.05	26.39
Lemon juice, raw	244	1.0 cup	54	0.85	16.84
Lime juice, raw	242	1.0 cup	60	1.02	20.38
Litchis, raw	190	1.0 cup	125	1.58	31.41
Loganberries, frozen	147	1.0 cup, unthawed	81	2.23	19.14
Longans, dried	1.7	1.0 fruit	5	0.08	1.26
Mangos, raw	165	1.0 cup pieces	99	1.35	24.72
Olives, pickled, canned or bottled, green	2.7	1.0 olive	4	0.03	0.1
Olives, ripe, canned (small-extra large)	8.4	1.0 tbsp	10	0.07	0.53
Orange juice, chilled, includes from concentrate, with added calcium	249	1.0 cup	117	1.69	28.06

Orange juice, chilled, includes from concentrate, with added calcium and vitamin D	249	1.0 cup	117	1.69	28.06
Orange juice, frozen concentrate, unsweetened, undiluted	262	1.0 cup	388	6.29	92.2
Orange peel, raw	6	1.0 tbsp	6	0.09	1.5
Oranges, raw, California, valencias	180	1.0 cup sections, without membranes	88	1.87	21.4
Oranges, raw, with peel	170	1.0 cup	107	2.21	26.35
Papaya, canned, heavy syrup, drained	39	1.0 piece	80	0.05	21.77
Papayas, raw	145	1.0 cup 1" pieces	62	0.68	15.69
Passion-fruit, (granadilla), purple, raw	236	1.0 cup	229	5.19	55.18
Peaches, canned, extra heavy syrup pack, solids and liquids	262	1.0 cup, halves or slices	252	1.23	68.28
Peaches, canned, light syrup pack, solids and liquids	251	1.0 cup, halves or slices	136	1.13	36.52
Peaches, canned, water pack, solids and liquids	244	1.0 cup, halves or slices	59	1.07	14.91
Peaches, dehydrated (low-moisture), sulfured, stewed	242	1.0 cup	322	4.86	82.62
Pears, canned, light syrup pack, solids and liquids	251	1.0 cup, halves	143	0.48	38.08
Pears, dried, sulfured, stewed, without added sugar	255	1.0 cup, halves	324	2.32	86.22
Pears, raw	140	1.0 cup, slices	80	0.5	21.32
Persimmons, japanese, raw	168	1.0 fruit (2-1/2" dia)	118	0.97	31.23
Plantains, cooked	200	1.0 cup, mashed	232	1.58	62.3
Plantains, raw	148	1.0 cup, sliced	181	1.92	47.2
Pomegranate juice, bottled	249	1.0 cup	134	0.37	32.69
Rowal, raw	114	0.5 cup	127	2.62	27.25
Tamarind nectar, canned	251	1.0 cup	143	0.23	36.97
Tangerines, (mandarin oranges), raw	195	1.0 cup, sections	103	1.58	26.01

Snacks

Description	Weight (g)	Measure	Energy (kcal)	Protein (g)	Carbohydrate, by difference (g)
Popcorn, sugar syrup/caramel, fat-free	28.4	1.0 oz	108	0.57	25.53
Snacks, corn-based, extruded, onion-flavor	28.4	1.0 oz	141	2.18	18.46
Snacks, corn-based, extruded, puffs or twists, cheese-flavor	28.4	1.0 oz, crunchy (about 21 pieces)	161	1.55	15.46
Snacks, crisped rice bar, chocolate chip	28	1.0 bar (1 oz)	113	1.43	20.44
Snacks, GENERAL MILLS, CHEX MIX, traditional flavor	28.4	1.0 oz	121	2.5	21.46
Snacks, granola bars, soft, uncoated, peanut butter	28	1.0 bar (1 oz)	119	2.94	18.03
Snacks, KELLOGG, KELLOGG'S RICE KRISPIES TREATS Squares	22	1.0 serving	91	0.75	17.71
Snacks, oriental mix, rice-based	28.4	1.0 oz	143	4.91	14.63
Snacks, pork skins, barbecue-flavor	28.4	1.0 oz	153	16.41	0.45

Snacks, potato chips, barbecue-flavor	28.4	1.0 oz	138	1.85	15.85
Snacks, potato chips, fat free, salted	28.4	1.0 oz	107	2.73	23.75
Snacks, potato chips, fat-free, made with olestra	28.4	1.0 oz	78	2.19	18.43
Snacks, potato chips, made from dried potatoes, cheese-flavor	28.4	1.0 oz	156	1.98	14.35
Snacks, potato chips, made from dried potatoes, fat-free, made with olestra	28.4	1.0 oz	72	1.43	15.88
Snacks, potato sticks	28.4	1.0 oz	148	1.9	15.11
Snacks, pretzels, hard, whole-wheat including both salted and unsalted	28.4	1.0 oz	103	3.15	23.05
Snacks, rice cakes, brown rice, buckwheat	9	1.0 cake	34	0.81	7.21
Snacks, rice cakes, brown rice, corn	9	1.0 cake	35	0.76	7.31
Snacks, rice cakes, brown rice, multigrain	9	1.0 cake	35	0.77	7.21
Snacks, tortilla chips, low fat, made with olestra, nacho cheese	28.4	1.0 oz	90	2.39	18.49
Snacks, tortilla chips, nacho-flavor, reduced fat	28.4	1.0 oz	126	2.47	20.3
Snacks, tortilla chips, ranch-flavor	28.4	1.0 oz	142	2.04	17.79
Snacks, trail mix, regular, with chocolate chips, unsalted nuts and seeds	146	1.0 cup	707	20.73	65.55

Sweets					
Description	Weight (g)	Measure	Energy (kcal)	Protein (g)	Carbohydrate, by difference(g)
Baking chocolate, MARS SNACKFOOD US, M & M's Milk Chocolate Mini Baking Bits	14	1.0 serving 0.5 oz, about 1 tbsp	70	0.67	9.58
Baking chocolate, MARS SNACKFOOD US, M & M's Semiswect Chocolate Mini Baking Bits	14	1.0 serving 0.5 oz, about 1 tbsp	72	0.62	9.23
Candies, 5TH AVENUE Candy Bar	56	1.0 bar 2 oz	270	4.92	35.1
Candies, caramels, chocolate-flavor roll	6.6	1.0 piece	26	0.1	5.79
Candies, chocolate, dark, NFS (45-59% cacao solids 90%; 60-69% cacao solids 5%; 70-85% cacao solids 5%)	28.4	1.0 oz	156	1.44	17
Candies, confectioner's coating, peanut butter	168	1.0 cup chips	889	30.74	78.76
Candies, dark chocolate coated coffee beans	40	1.0 serving 28 pieces	216	3	23.98
Candies, fudge, chocolate, with nuts, prepared-from-recipe	28.4	1.0 oz	131	1.24	19.26
Candies, HERSHEY'S, ALMOND JOY BITES	40	18.0 pieces	225	2.23	23.02
Candies, HERSHEY, KIT KAT BIG KAT Bar	55	1.0 bar 1.94 oz	286	3.43	35
Candies, MARS SNACKFOOD US, 3 MUSKETEERS Bar	60	1.0 serving 2.13 oz bar	262	1.56	46.66
Candies, MARS SNACKFOOD US, M & M's Milk Chocolate Candies	48	1.0 package (1.69 oz)	236	2.08	34.17
Candies, MARS SNACKFOOD US, POPABLES SNICKERS Brand Bite Size Candies	39	1.0 serving 13 pieces	187	2.79	23.82
Candies, MARS SNACKFOOD US, STARBURST Fruit Chews, Original fruits	40	1.0 serving fun size (8 chews)	163	0.16	33.03
Candies, MOUNDS Candy Bar	19	1.0 bar snack size	92	0.87	11.13
Candies, NESTLE, 100 GRAND Bar	43	1.0 bar (1.5 oz)	201	1.07	30.52

125

Candies, NESTLE, BUTTERFINGER Bar	60	1.0 serving 2.1 oz bar	275	3.24	43.74
Candies, NESTLE, BUTTERFINGER Crisp	60	1.0 piece	279	4	41.07
Candies, NESTLE, CRUNCH Bar and Dessert Topping	44	1.0 bar 1.55 oz	220	2.2	29.48
Candies, truffles, prepared-from-recipe	12	1.0 piece	61	0.75	5.39
Candies, TWIZZLERS CHERRY BITES	40	18.0 pieces	135	1.19	31.75
Candies, YORK BITES	39	15.0 pieces	154	0.69	31.84
Candies, YORK Peppermint Pattie	43	1.0 patty 1.5 oz	165	0.94	34.83
Chocolate, dark, 60-69% cacao solids	28.4	1.0 oz	164	1.74	14.86
Chocolate-flavored hazelnut spread	37	1.0 serving 2 TBSP	200	2	23
Desserts, mousse, chocolate, prepared-from-recipe	808	1.0 recipe yield	1818	33.45	129.85
Flan, caramel custard, dry mix	85	1.0 package (3 oz)	296	0	77.86
Frostings, coconut-nut, ready-to-eat	38	0.083 package	165	0.57	20.03
Frostings, glaze, chocolate, prepared-from-recipe, with butter, NFSMI Recipe No. C-32	33	2.0 tablespoon	118	0.47	23.82
Frozen novelties, ice type, sugar free, orange, cherry, and grape POPSICLE pops	55	1.0 serving 1.75 fl oz pop	12	0	2.83
Frozen novelties, KLONDIKE, SLIM-A-BEAR Fudge Bar, 98% fat free, no sugar added	74	1.0 serving 3.5 fl oz bar	92	3.19	22.25
Frozen novelties, No Sugar Added, FUDGSICLE pops	84	1.0 serving	104	3.08	19.41
Gelatin desserts, dry mix, with added ascorbic acid, sodium-citrate and salt	85	1.0 package (3 oz)	324	6.63	76.92
Ice creams, BREYERS, All Natural Light French Chocolate	68	1.0 serving 1/2 cup	137	3.6	20.18
Ice creams, BREYERS, All Natural Light Mint Chocolate Chip	68	1.0 serving 1/2 cup	133	3.19	19.31
Ice creams, BREYERS, All Natural Light Vanilla	68	1.0 serving 1/2 cup	110	3.29	17.2
Ice creams, vanilla, light, no sugar added	68	1.0 serving 1/2 cup	115	2.7	14.57
Puddings, banana, dry mix, regular, with added oil	88	1.0 package (3.12 oz)	341	0	77.79
Puddings, chocolate, dry mix, regular, prepared with whole milk	142	0.5 cup	170	4.49	27.89
Puddings, chocolate, ready-to-eat	28.4	1.0 oz	40	0.59	6.52
Puddings, chocolate, ready-to-eat, fat free	113	1.0 serving 4 oz	105	2.18	23.58
Puddings, lemon, dry mix, regular, with added oil, potassium, sodium	85	1.0 package (3 oz)	311	0.09	76.75
Puddings, rice, ready-to-eat	113	1.0 serving 4 oz pudding cup	122	3.65	20.78
Puddings, tapioca, dry mix, with no added salt	92	1.0 package (3.5 oz)	339	0.09	86.76
Puddings, tapioca, ready-to-eat, fat free	112	1.0 container refrigerated 4 oz	105	1.61	23.87
Puddings, vanilla, dry mix, regular, with added oil	88	1.0 package (3.12 oz)	325	0.26	81.31
Snacks, fruit leather, rolls	21	1.0 large	78	0.02	18.02
Sweetener, herbal extract powder from Stevia leaf	1	1.0 package	--	0	1
Sweeteners, for baking, brown, contains sugar and sucralose	12.9	1.0 tbsp	50	0	12.53
Syrups, table blends, pancake	314	1.0 cup	735	0	193.02
Syrups, table blends, pancake, with 2% maple, with added potassium	315	1.0 cup	835	0	219.24

Beverages

Description	Weight (g)	Measure	Energy (kcal)	Protein (g)	Carbohydrate, by difference (g)
Alcoholic beverage, beer, light, BUD LIGHT	29.5	1.0 fl oz	9	0.07	0.38
Alcoholic beverage, daiquiri, canned	30.5	1.0 fl oz	38	0	4.79
Alcoholic beverage, liqueur, coffee, 63 proof	34.8	1.0 fl oz	107	0.03	11.21
Alcoholic beverage, pina colada, canned	32.6	1.0 fl oz	77	0.2	9
Alcoholic beverage, tequila sunrise, canned	31.1	1.0 fl oz	34	0.09	3.51
Alcoholic beverage, whiskey sour, canned	30.8	1.0 fl oz	37	0	4.13
Alcoholic Beverage, wine, table, red, Cabernet Franc	29.4	1.0 fl oz	24	0.02	0.72
Alcoholic Beverage, wine, table, red, Cabernet Sauvignon	29.4	1.0 fl oz	24	0.02	0.76
Alcoholic Beverage, wine, table, red, Claret	29.4	1.0 fl oz	24	0.02	0.88
Alcoholic Beverage, wine, table, red, Lemberger	29.4	1.0 fl oz	24	0.02	0.72
Alcoholic Beverage, wine, table, red, Petite Sirah	29.5	1.0 fl oz	25	0.02	0.79
Alcoholic beverage, wine, table, white	29.4	1.0 fl oz	24	0.02	0.76
Alcoholic beverage, wine, table, white, Chardonnay	29.3	1.0 fl oz	25	0.02	0.63
Alcoholic beverage, wine, table, white, Chenin Blanc	29.5	1.0 fl oz	24	0.02	0.98
Alcoholic beverage, wine, table, white, Muscat	30	1.0 fl oz	25	0.02	1.57
Alcoholic beverage, wine, table, white, Pinot Blanc	29.3	1.0 fl oz	24	0.02	0.57
Alcoholic beverage, wine, table, white, Riesling	29.6	1.0 fl oz	24	0.02	1.11
Alcoholic beverage, wine, table, white, Sauvignon Blanc	29.3	1.0 fl oz	24	0.02	0.6
Alcoholic beverage, wine, table, white, Semillon	29.5	1.0 fl oz	24	0.02	0.92
Beverages, almond milk, chocolate, ready-to-drink	240	8.0 fl oz	120	1.51	22.51
Beverages, almond milk, sweetened, vanilla flavor, ready-to-drink	240	8.0 fl oz	91	1.01	15.82
Beverages, carbonated, club soda	29.6	1.0 fl oz	--	0	--
Beverages, carbonated, low calorie, cola or pepper-type, with aspartame, contains caffeine	29.6	1.0 fl oz	1	0.03	0.09
Beverages, carbonated, low calorie, other than cola or pepper, with aspartame, contains caffeine	29.6	1.0 fl oz	--	0.03	0
Beverages, carbonated, reduced sugar, cola, contains caffeine and sweeteners	29.6	1.0 fl oz	6	0	1.53
Beverages, chocolate powder, no sugar added	11	2.0 tbsp	41	1	7
Beverages, coffee substitute, cereal grain beverage, prepared with water	30.1	1.0 fl oz	2	0.03	0.39
Beverages, coffee, instant, decaffeinated, powder	1.8	1.0 tsp rounded	6	0.21	1.37

Beverages, cranberry-apricot juice drink, bottled	30.6	1.0 fl oz	20	0.06	4.96
Beverages, cranberry-grape juice drink, bottled	30.6	1.0 fl oz	17	0.06	4.28
Beverages, Energy drink, AMP, sugar free	240	8.0 fl oz	5	0	2.47
Beverages, Energy drink, ROCKSTAR, sugar free	240	8.0 fl oz	10	0.6	1.68
Beverages, Meal supplement drink, canned, peanut flavor	158	1.0 cup	160	5.53	23.29
Beverages, Orange drink, breakfast type, with juice and pulp, frozen concentrate	36.3	1.0 fl oz	56	0.15	14.16
Beverages, Propel Zero, fruit-flavored, non-carbonated	29.6	1.0 fl oz	1	0	0.34
Beverages, Protein powder soy based	45	1.0 scoop	175	25	13
Beverages, tea, instant, unsweetened, powder	0.7	1.0 serving 1 tsp	2	0.14	0.41
Beverages, The COCA-COLA company, Hi-C Flashin' Fruit Punch	200	6.75 fl oz	90	0	25
Beverages, THE COCA-COLA COMPANY, NOS energy drink, Original, grape, loaded cherry, charged citrus, fortified with vitamins B6 and B12	480	16.0 fl oz	211	0	54
Beverages, UNILEVER, SLIMFAST, meal replacement, regular, ready-to-drink, 3-2-1 Plan	295	1.0 bottle	168	9.79	22.83
Beverages, V8 SPLASH Juice Drinks, Diet Tropical Blend	238	1.0 serving 8 oz	10	0	3
Beverages, V8 SPLASH Juice Drinks, Mango Peach	243	1.0 serving 8 oz	80	0	20
Beverages, V8 SPLASH Smoothies, Peach Mango	245	1.0 serving 8 oz	91	2.99	19.01
Beverages, V8 SPLASH Smoothies, Strawberry Banana	245	1.0 serving 8 oz	91	2.99	19.99
Beverages, V8 V-FUSION Juices, Peach Mango	246	1.0 serving 8 oz	121	1.01	27.99
Beverages, water, bottled, non-carbonated, CALISTOGA	29.6	1.0 fl oz	--	0	--
Beverages, water, bottled, non-carbonated, EVIAN	29.6	1.0 fl oz	--	0	--
Beverages, Whey protein powder isolate	86	3.0 scoop	309	50	25
Beverages, Whiskey sour mix, bottled	32.3	1.0 fl oz	28	0.03	6.91
Water, bottled, non-carbonated, NAYA	29.6	1.0 fl oz	--	0	--
Whiskey sour mix, bottled, with added potassium and sodium	32.3	1.0 fl oz	27	0.03	6.91

Source : USDA (2017)

Calories Burned in 1 Hour
for Different Physical Activities

Activity (1-hour duration)	Weight of person and calories burned		
	160 pounds (73 kilograms)	**200 pounds (91 kilograms)**	**240 pounds (109 kilograms)**
Aerobics, high impact	533	664	796
Aerobics, low impact	365	455	545
Aerobics, water	402	501	600
Backpacking	511	637	763
Basketball game	584	728	872
Bicycling, < 10 mph, leisure	292	364	436
Bowling	219	273	327
Canoeing	256	319	382
Dancing, ballroom	219	273	327
Elliptical trainer, moderate effort	365	455	545
Football, touch or flag	584	728	872
Golfing, carrying clubs	314	391	469
Hiking	438	546	654
Ice skating	511	637	763
Racquetball	511	637	763
Resistance (weight) training	365	455	545
Rollerblading	548	683	818
Rope jumping	861	1,074	1,286
Rowing, stationary	438	546	654
Running, 5 mph	606	755	905
Running, 8 mph	861	1,074	1,286
Skiing, cross-country	496	619	741
Skiing, downhill	314	391	469
Skiing, water	438	546	654
Softball or baseball	365	455	545
Stair treadmill	657	819	981
Swimming laps, light or moderate	423	528	632
Swimming laps, vigorous	715	892	1,068
Tae kwon do	752	937	1,123
Tai chi	219	273	327
Tennis, singles	584	728	872
Volleyball	292	364	436
Walking, 2 mph	204	255	305
Walking, 3.5 mph	314	391	469
Yoga, hatha	183	228	273
Yoga, power	292	364	436

Source: Mayo Clinic

Tips For Dieting Success

Even if you are armed with the best recipes, there are certain habits that you must adopt if your diet is going to be a success. Some of these are lifestyle adjustments; others are about shifting your thought patterns or changing lifelong bad habits. If you are part of a weight loss support group, you likely already have an arsenal of tips for success, but this is one area that you can never have too much of. Here are a few simple tips for long term success with your healthy eating and weight loss goals.

1. Drink more water. It is impossible to be your healthiest self if you are not properly hydrated. Water is vital for practically every function of your body. Plus, sometimes hunger cues are really just your body telling you that you are thirsty. Keep a glass or bottle of water with you throughout the day to quench thirst and fight off unnecessary cravings.

2. Divide foods up into smaller portion sizes as soon as you get home from the grocery store, preferably when you are not hungry. Foods such as cheese or nuts are nutritious, but also calorie dense and very easy to overindulge in. On the other hand, cut up vegetables offer a low calorie, healthy option that will fill you up. When you open up your refrigerator to reach for a snack, go ahead and have the cheese, just grab one of the small snacking portions that you have prepared. You might also look at the entire bowl of salad that you can have instead and choose the more filling option.

3. Add exciting new life to your favorite foods by adding different herbs. If you have always wanted to try a herb, but never had the occasion to do so, now is the time. Choose fresh herbs whenever possible. They pack more of a flavor punch and on an emotional level feel more indulgent. Some herbs are more potent than others, so it is best to do some preliminary research online to know which herbs you should use in moderation.

4. Listen to your body. Think about all of the times that your body leads you in the right direction if you are willing to trust it. A toddler will binge on fruit when they need vitamin C. A pregnant woman might crave steak if she needs iron. If you are craving something sweet, don't just shrug that craving aside, but modify how you satisfy the ne. Instead of ice cream, choose a nondairy alternative. Instead erry pie, indulge in a bowl of berries with a little bit of whipped and nut crumble. Instead of the chocolate cake, sit down with e of dark chocolate and savor the intensity of the flavor. Do of your cravings that can be classified as "unhealthy".

5. Portion control is crucial. Learn to recognize what three ounces of meat or one cup of pasta looks like. Invest in a food scale and accurate measuring utensils and measure everything, especially until you feel that you can recognize an appropriately sized portion.

6. Start with small steps. Begin by adding a healthy portion of vegetables to your lunch time sandwich. Next time, scale back a little on the meat or cheese. After that, trade out fattening condiments such as mayo for mustard, etc. We are trained to resist too much change, which is a trap for losing control of your diet. Making small little changes that eventually lead up to big ones will help to ensure long term success.

7. Make it a goal to try one new healthy food or recipe each week. This will give you something to look forward to and expand the diversity of your options.

8. Make meal or snack time a priority. This means shutting out all other distractions and not multitasking. Don't eat at your desk while you are working. Turn off your phone when you sit down for the family dinner and don't eat in front of the television. Being distracted and multitasking takes away from the pleasurable experience of eating and can result in consuming more calories throughout the day.

9. If you are having a hard time giving up a "forbidden" food, try to come up with an alternative. If you love mayonnaise, there are plenty of low-fat options available. If you crave fruit flavored sodas, try a sparkling water with a little fruit juice or fresh fruit added.

10. Speak up for yourself. Some people make sticking to your goals more difficult. Sometimes it is intentional, while other times people are well meaning, but uninformed. You cannot expect anyone to respect your goals if you do not make them known and let people know explicitly what is or isn't helpful. Tell grandmother that you love her cookies, but will not have more than one. Tell your coworkers that you cannot join them for lunch if they choose a place that doesn't offer any healthy alternatives, etc.

Made in the USA
Middletown, DE
30 December 2017